Exploring the Weather

Exploring the Weather

Brian Clegg

VIVAYS PUBLISHING

Dedication

For Gillian, Rebecca and Chelsea.

Published by Vivays Publishing Ltd
www.vivays-publishing.com

© 2013 Brian Clegg

A catalogue record for this book is available from the British Library

ISBN 978-1-908126-43-6

Publishing Director: Lee Ripley
Designer: Nick Newton

Cover: Keith Kent/Science Photo Library
Frontispiece: © Jerry Greenberg/Science Photo Library

Printed in China

Contents

Introduction   6

Chapter 1   Predicting the inevitable   14

Chapter 2   Weather goes scientific   32

Chapter 3   Cloud cover   48

Chapter 4   The power of the Sun   64

Chapter 5   Rain, rain   72

Chapter 6   The white stuff   84

Chapter 7   Hurricanes, cyclones and typhoons   100

Chapter 8   Drought   114

Chapter 9   Tornadoes   130

Chapter 10   It's electrifying   138

Chapter 11   Weather from space   150

Chapter 12   Challenging the climate   162

Epilogue   The wonder of weather   176

Picture credits   186

Index   187

Introduction

I'm from England. One of the strongest national stereotypes about British people is that we are obsessed with the weather. And there's an element of truth in it. If all else fails, if conversation is faltering, we will instantly resort to commenting how cold or wet or hot the weather has been of late.

'Surprisingly warm for the time of year.'
'Yes, but it looks like rain later.'

Yet this fascination us Brits have with the weather should hardly come as a surprise to anyone. After all, weather can all too easily make the difference between plenty and famine, survival and death. This is not a topic any human being can afford to ignore.

According to my dictionary, 'weather' refers to the condition of the atmosphere at a particular place and time (as opposed to climate, which has a wider span). As I write this, for example, the weather in Swindon, England, is sunny and dry with clear blue skies, but it is bitingly cold as it is still winter. The climate here, on the other hand, is mild with a tendency to wetness.

Although the official definition of the weather focuses only on the state of the Earth's atmosphere, which makes it seem limited to the behaviour of a few gases swirling above us, isolated from our existence on the solid surface of the planet, the reality is very different. Weather is as much about what that atmosphere can throw at us on the ground, and about the impact it will have on our bodies, crops and habitat, as it is about the state of the air.

We take the atmosphere for granted. It seems little more than the layer of gas stuck to the outside of the planet. But this layer forms a complex system – which is why meteorology, the science of predicting the weather, is anything but easy.

The atmosphere itself is a mixture of gases. Oxygen, that familiar gas essential for breathing, makes up around 21 percent, while the dominant constituent is the relatively inert nitrogen at 78 percent. Throw in a number of other gases (notably argon and carbon dioxide), plus water both as vapour and droplets, and a host of particles from soot to bacteria and you have the constituents for the blanket that surrounds our planet. But this is anything but a homogenous mix.

The atmosphere is divided into five layers, only one of which has a commonly used name – the stratosphere. This forms the second layer up (hence the use of the word to indicate reaching dizzy heights) – the bottom layer that we live in is called the troposphere. We stay in the troposphere for around the first 18 kilometres (11 miles) at sea level, reducing to as little as 10 kilometres (6 miles) in mountainous regions.

The troposphere is where the vast majority of the weather happens. Because the atmosphere gets thinner as you get further away from the Earth (an inevitable result of the fact that gravity falls off with distance, and it's gravity that holds the atmosphere in place), around 75 percent of all the gas in the atmosphere is within the troposphere, and 90 percent of the atmosphere's mass. As you head up through this deep layer, temperatures fall to around -80°C (-112°F). But at the top of the troposphere, a boundary known as the tropopause, temperature stops dropping with height and starts to rise instead. This change means that we have reached the stratosphere.

The stratosphere contains most of our atmosphere's ozone, a relatively unusual variant of oxygen that has three atoms per molecule instead of the usual two (its chemical formula is O_3). Ozone is present

The Earth's atmosphere from space

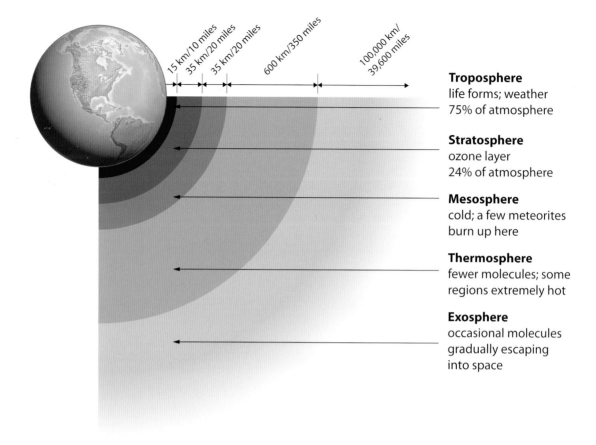

15 km/10 miles
35 km/20 miles
35 km/20 miles
600 km/350 miles
100,000 km/ 39,600 miles

Troposphere
life forms; weather
75% of atmosphere

Stratosphere
ozone layer
24% of atmosphere

Mesosphere
cold; a few meteorites
burn up here

Thermosphere
fewer molecules; some
regions extremely hot

Exosphere
occasional molecules
gradually escaping
into space

in the metallic tang of an electrical discharge and is highly poisonous, so it's just as well that it's tucked away up in the stratosphere.

Up there, the O_3 gas is good at absorbing the energetic ultraviolet rays of the Sun, which is why the hole in the ozone layer caused such concern, as any extra ultraviolet getting through would significantly increase the incidence of skin cancer and ultraviolet based problems. This absorption of incoming energy from the Sun results in the stratosphere being able to retain its temperature, despite there being less of a blanket of air above to keep it warm than there is above the troposphere.

At the top of the stratosphere, through the boundary called the stratopause, we reach the mesosphere. With little ozone here to latch on to energetic light, the temperature starts to fall away with height again, in a layer that can reach as far as 87 kilometres (54 miles) above the Earth's surface. This is the coldest layer of the atmosphere as it lacks the ability to hold warmth in.

Atmospheric layers

The atmosphere is now getting very thin as we reach the thermosphere. With unprotected exposure to sunlight, temperatures begin to soar at this point, reaching as high as 15,000°C (27,000°F), nearly three times the temperature of the surface of the Sun. And then comes the final extremity, the exosphere, where the remaining components get thinner and thinner, mostly composed of light gases like hydrogen on their way into space.

There is no clear point at which the atmosphere ends. You can't specify where the edge of it is – the pull of gravity goes on effectively for ever, as witness the fact that it holds the Moon in place around 380,000 kilometres (235,000 miles) away. But that pull drops off with the square of the distance. Get far enough out and you need something as massive as a moon to get enough mutual attraction. A few molecules of gas don't stand a chance. The limit of the exosphere is generally put at approximately 100,000 kilometres (62,000 miles).

The Earth's weather is certainly gentle if we compare it with some of our neighbours in the Solar System. On Venus, for example, vast electrical storms rend the sulphuric acid clouds over thousands of square miles, while Jupiter has downpours of glowing pink neon rain and a cyclone bigger than the entire planet Earth forming the Great Red Spot. This giant storm has been raging for over 200 years. But though our weather is much milder than these planetary extremes, we are totally dependent on weather systems for our survival. And it would be unfair to call it dull – whether we're thinking of the everyday basics of rain and sun, wind and cloud, or the many dramatic moments the weather brings.

At its best, weather is something to celebrate: the perfect blue skies of a summer holiday; the moment of awe when you pull back the curtains and everything is covered in a pristine blanket of snow; or the coming of life-giving rains after a drought. At its worst, the extreme phenomena of storms, winds and flood bring misery and death. But most of the time we exist somewhere in between. We take the weather for granted, moaning about another day of rain, or half-noticing a pretty cloud formation without really taking it in.

Recently we have also started to take note of the weather's big brother: climate. Considering climate moves us away from a particular locale in time and space, instead giving us the bigger picture

over years or decades, perhaps for a continent or for the whole world. The topic of climate change – what is happening, what is driving it, whether it has a significant manmade component – is as much a concern for politics as it is a part of science. Yet it's impossible to look at weather without thinking about climate change and its implications.

Weather and climate take the activity of invisible gases and turn them into remarkable visual spectacles. Most of the time we take the weather for granted. But the images in this book should remind us that weather is a subject that is always ready to fascinate and delight.

The solar system's most impressive storm – the Great Red Spot on Jupiter

Chapter 1

Predicting the inevitable

As physicist Niels Bohr once said, 'Prediction is very difficult, especially about the future.' This difficulty with foreseeing the future is not always true for science. We can, for example, predict exactly when Halley's Comet will return and sweep around the Sun on its 75-year orbit (the next time it will be sighted from the ground will be in 2061), but we are incapable of forecasting the weather more than a few days ahead. Knowing how the weather is going to develop is incredibly important, whether we want to travel by air and sea, plant crops or just have a good day out without getting soaked. But how can we know the future when dealing with something as intangible as this?

Forecasting how the weather will change is a challenge that has been faced for as long as human beings have thought about nature and how it works. Originally, predicting the weather was a subject largely left to the priest or the shaman. At first sight, what they did

appears to be not so much a prediction as an attempt at weather control. The idea was to intercede with the gods who were thought to inflict the weather on the people of the Earth as a reward or punishment for their actions.

In practice, though, a savvy priest would indeed be adept at spotting signs that helped predict the weather. If he or she had a fair idea of what was coming they could then claim to be asking the gods to bring bad weather as a punishment or good weather as a reward. Get the prediction right and they seemed to wield enormous power, keeping the priesthood safe in their position of knowledge.

This supernatural view of the weather as being something caused by gods, spirits or magic would last well into the medieval period, when witches would sometimes be blamed for bringing on a patch of bad weather that damaged an enemy's crops (something that sadly can still happen in modern-day Africa). As with many topics, one of the first to think scientifically about the weather was the Greek philosopher Aristotle. Living between 384 and 322 BC, Aristotle was almost always wrong about science – but in a sense that doesn't matter.

The problem with science in Aristotle's time is that it worked more like the law does today than a true science. Instead of relying on experiment and careful observation to decide the most likely scientific explanation for a phenomenon like the weather, different theories would be debated, and whichever idea did best in debate would be accepted as the truth, even if it bore no resemblance to reality. Famously, Aristotle opined that women had fewer teeth than men. He never bothered to check and people just took his word for it.

Aristotle's scientific legacy was not so much the accuracy of his theories, as his ability to set the agenda. He covered a vast range of subjects that science would come back to again and again. Some topics were fairly abstract, like the nature of infinity, but others were very practical, with significance for the everyday lives of everyone. And one of these topics was forecasting the weather.

Aristotle explored one of the fundamental components of the weather system: the flow of water through the atmosphere and around the world. He described how water evaporates from bodies of water like oceans and lakes, is carried through the air by the wind and then falls elsewhere as rain. This idea was in a book, which he called

Aristotle's weather system focused on water flows

Meteorologica, the word from which we get the unfortunately clumsy name 'meteorology' for the study and forecasting of the weather. It sounds like it should be about meteors, but it originally just meant the study of things that are raised up and lofty – in essence what goes on in the air (though in Aristotle's original version it also extended out into space, so did include those meteors).

The ancient Greeks were largely interested in describing nature, exploring its qualities rather than applying any kind of quantitative

The Tower of the Winds, Athens

measure. So, for instance, like many early cultures they used wind vanes to see how the wind varied in direction, but they didn't think about making a numerical measurement of its speed. Probably the best-known surviving piece of Greek weather technology is the Tower of the Winds, a 12-metre (40-foot) high structure in Athens, devised by the astronomer Andonikos around 50 BC and originally topped with an ornate weather vane.

It wasn't really until the 17th century that Renaissance thinkers began to look for ways to make direct measurements to pin down exactly what the weather was doing. How much rain had fallen? How fast was the wind blowing? How did the temperature vary through the day? Was there any relationship between the air pressure and what was happening to the weather? Were there any regular patterns, so once you knew the behaviour of the weather in a particular place, you could predict how it would change in the future?

As basic science began to explain the relationship between temperature, pressure and volume of a gas like the air – and at the same time instrument makers added thermometers and barometers to the armoury of would-be weather forecasters – it became possible for the first time to get a feeling for what the weather was actually doing at the moment and from this to make a realistic stab at predicting how the weather was going to change in the future.

It's not that attempts hadn't been made before. Folk weather forecasting made use of (and still does make use of) cloud patterns, plants, seaweed and the behaviour of animals and birds to predict what was likely to come. Most people are familiar with the rhyme 'Red sky at night, shepherd's delight; red sky at morning, shepherd's warning,' suggesting that good weather followed a red sky around dusk (producing happy shepherds), but a red sky at dawn was likely to presage a storm. There is an element of truth in this.

Red sky at night

Red skies occur for the same reason the setting sun appears red and the sky unencumbered with clouds generally appears blue – because of the scattering of sunlight. Generally the molecules of the air (and dust particles) scatter more blue light than red, the result being a blue sky because the blue light from the Sun is less likely to come directly to your eye and more likely to take a roundabout trip across the sky.

With the bluer aspects of its light extracted and sent off on an excursion through the atmosphere, the near-white Sun appears yellow in the day and red in the evening, when the light has to go through more air because of the shallower angle of its rays, producing a greater amount of scattering. Red skies most frequently come with high pressure, which has a tendency to trap more particles in the air. High pressure is more likely to turn up at night if it is moving into a region, while high pressure in the morning is more often on its way out. As high pressure over an area tends to make for better weather, this results in a degree of success for the folk prediction.

There are also certain types of clouds that have been used to forecast what's on the way with some good cause. Of course sighting a huge thunderhead moving in isn't exactly rocket science, nor is the link between blackness in the clouds and rain, but there are more subtle indicators. Altocumulus clouds in a pattern rather like lines of fish scales (sometimes called a mackerel sky) and comma-shaped high cirrus clouds, known as mares' tails, both indicate a good chance of high winds on the way, as these clouds often form in advance of a storm.

Relying on nature for short-lived local forecasts is not without merit. It is still said today that if cows are lying down during the day it is likely to rain, because they prefer not to lie on wet grass, so get settled before the rainfall sets in. They do often seem to read the signs well, though there are plenty of other reasons a herd of cattle could decide to settle down other than an impending downpour. Similarly, swallows are said to presage stormy weather if they fly low. As storms are often accompanied by strong winds at the higher altitudes where swallows tend to fly, these winds can force the birds to fly lower, so they act as high-level wind speed detectors.

Mares' tails

Similarly, the traditional use of seaweed and pinecones as weather forecasting instruments has a degree of logic. When the humidity – the amount of water vapour in the air – is high, some seaweeds have a noticeably different feel. They are more floppy and less dry, while pinecones open up to reveal their seeds. The assumption is (as can sometimes be the case) that this increase in humidity could be a warning that rain is on the way.

Long-term predictions from nature were also undertaken regularly in folk forecasting, but these were very unlikely to have any value. All sorts of natural occurrences were said to come before a bad winter. Animals that store up food for the winter, like squirrels, were said to build a particularly big supply. Insects that undertake building projects like ants and termites were thought to produce particularly large structures before a bad winter, while trees were supposed to produce more berries than usual.

There's a sort of logic here if the animals and plants were given a forewarning. These are actions you could imagine them taking if they truly knew that there was a bad winter on the way. But in practice there seems to be very little evidence for a link between these happenings and how the weather will turn out. This is a classic example of the kind of selective observation that science tries to eliminate. Those using such long-term forecasts would tend to remember when they were right but ignore them when they were wrong, confirming the feeling that surely there was something behind them.

Even worse than long-term nature forecasts, are forecasts based on legend. In the UK it is often said that if it rains on St Swithun's Day (July 15th), then it will rain for 40 days. Swithun was a bishop of Winchester in England who died in 862. His grave, at his request, was in a humble location where the rain could fall on it. But in 971 his remains were dug up and moved into the cathedral. This is said to have been followed by 40 days and nights of rain, supposedly showing the saint's displeasure at being moved and leading to the tradition.

In reality this prediction seems to have been constructed to make a good story – there is no evidence of such torrential weather at the time – and it's more likely that there happened to be a season of downpours following one St Swithun's Day that started the tradition. As it happens, July 15th is roughly when the jet stream influencing weather in the UK tends to settle into a pattern that holds for several weeks – but there is clearly no reason why the saint should cause the weather.

There's a similar wet period expected in France and Hungary if it rains on Saint Médard's (Medardus) Day – June 8th. This is probably connected with an old tradition about Médard, a sixth-century bishop of Vermandois in northeast France. It is said that he was once sheltered from a downpour by an eagle which hovered over him with open wings. These kinds of predictions are obviously based on superstition rather than any true weather lore.

Perhaps the most colourful weather superstition is the US tradition of Groundhog Day. Taking place on February 2nd, the legend has it that the actions of a groundhog coming out of its burrow determine the weather for the following six weeks. If it is overcast and the groundhog casts no shadow then there will be an early spring. But if it's sunny, and the groundhog sees its shadow, it will flee back into its burrow, bringing on six weeks of wintry weather.

This tradition seems to have come over from Germany (where a badger took the leading role) with the Pennsylvania 'Dutch', settlers

of German origin (that's Deutsch, meaning German, not Dutch, from Holland). Its origins seem linked to the Christian festival of Candlemas (or the Presentation of Jesus at the Temple) which takes place on the same date. Celebrated in Pennsylvania since the 19th century and spread since to Canada, Groundhog Day makes for a quaint day's entertainment – but despite claims to the contrary from the organizers of the events, the groundhog's weather predictions are hopeless, getting things right or wrong at random.

Meteorologists, of course, tend to give more attention to instruments than they do to groundhogs. In a modern ground-based weather station, much the same instruments are likely to be seen in action as have been in use for the last two hundred years, though the technology for detecting and recording changes will usually be electronic these days. You often still see weather stations located in boxes on legs that look a little like beehives. These boxes are 'Stevenson Screens' which are devised to keep the instruments in as controlled an environment as possible. They are named after their designer, Thomas Stevenson, the engineer father of author Robert Louis Stevenson.

Many of the measurements necessary for weather forecasting are obvious and everyday. Temperature, for example, measured with a

thermometer, is something with which we are all familiar. Technically, temperature is a measure of the kinetic energy of the molecules in something. So, for instance, the air temperature is a measure of how fast the air molecules are zooming about. The faster they go, the more energy they have (think of the difference between being hit by a ball travelling at five miles per hour and 50 miles per hour). When the air molecules have higher energy, the air has a higher temperature. But in practice, we all know that the temperature tells us how hot or cold it feels.

What is less agreed on is what units to use in measuring temperature. The traditional units were on the Fahrenheit scale, which has the rather bizarre temperatures of 32° and 212° for the freezing and boiling points of water respectively. These strange numbers came about because the scale was mostly set using temperatures unrelated to water. Zero was defined as the temperature of a mix of ice, water and the chemical ammonium chloride. This odd combination was chosen because it is relatively easy to keep it at a fixed temperature. The German physicist Daniel Fahrenheit, who dreamed up the scale, then added two points for the freezing point of water and the temperature of the human body. These were set at 32° and 96°.

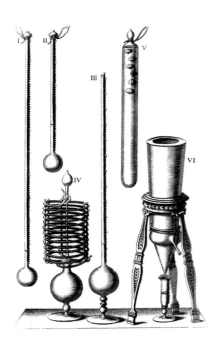

Early thermometers

While these still sound like strange values to select, there was a degree of logic to the choice. The reasoning was that the difference between these two handy temperature limits was 64, and as this is a power of two, it's easy to split up a length 64 times by repeated halving. The boiling point of water simply didn't come into the equation – it just happens to be 212°.

The Celsius scale on the other hand, widely used in science and the norm in most parts of the world other than the US, sets 0° and 100° as the freezing and boiling points of water respectively, which seems decidedly more straightforward. (The original version of the scale, named after Swedish astronomer Anders Celsius, had 0° as the boiling point and 100° as the freezing point, just to cause confusion.)

As if this weren't complicated enough, scientists often use a third temperature measure, the Kelvin scale. This has the same size units as Celsius, but instead of starting at the freezing point of water, it starts at absolute zero. Temperature has a starting point, the ultimate in coldness. Once you know that temperature is a measure of the average speed of atoms, it has to have a lower limit, absolute zero, where the speed of the atoms is zero.

In practice absolute zero isn't possible to reach, as quantum particles like atoms can never be entirely still. Absolute zero is around -273.15 °C, making the freezing point of water 273.15 K. Unlike the other two scales, the Kelvin scale uses the unit kelvins, and doesn't have the clumsy 'degrees' we associate with temperature, a word that originally just meant a step, so a degree is a step up or down in the level of heat.

Like temperature, wind speed is a fairly obvious meteorological measurement. This describes the rate at which a particular section of air is moving with respect to the ground. Air molecules are moving all the time. Even with no wind at all they hurtle backwards and forwards, constantly colliding and changing direction. But wind speed measures how a body of air moves, averaging out all those darting motions to provide an overall shift in a block of air molecules in a particular direction.

Wind speed is usually measured with an anemometer, an instrument that has cups like half tennis balls fixed to the end of rods that rotate with the wind that is caught in the cups. The faster the

An anemometer

wind blows, the faster the rods are pushed around. Combined with a weather vane to indicate the direction the wind is blowing, a modern anemometer, usually mounted around 10 metres (33 feet) in the air, is not much different from the early versions, merely using electronics to record and collect the results.

Again, wind speed seems a natural measure, because we can feel the impact of the wind, and can see its action when it makes tree leaves flutter or objects blow around. It is clearly important to know the wind speed, not only to warn of the wind's impact, but also because it gives information about the rate at which weather phenomena are moving from place to place. Admittedly, all of the air doesn't move at the same speed – there can be a much faster wind carrying clouds along than is detected at 10 metres above the ground – but monitoring the way that the wind speed changes is an essential contribution to understanding the development of weather patterns.

It is also useful to know how humid the air is, which will have a direct effect on the amount of precipitation that takes place. We might not have a natural feel for the quantification of humidity, but the idea of air being more or less humid – in effect holding more or less water in the air – is a natural one. Humidity is traditionally measured indirectly, using a hygrometer. This consists of two thermometers, one with a normal, dry bulb, but the other with a bulb that is kept moist.

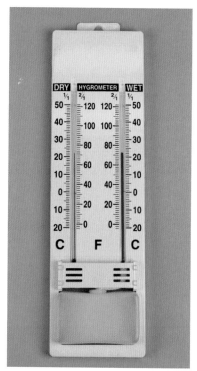

Wet and dry bulb hygrometer

A Campbell-Stokes sunshine recorder

The rate of evaporation of the water influences the temperature the thermometer shows – and that rate is controlled by the humidity in the air. When a liquid evaporates it takes energy from its surroundings, cooling down anything in contact. This is why sweating cools us down (and how a fan keeps us cool). The higher the humidity, the slower the water will evaporate and so there will be less difference in temperature. Modern measurements of humidity may use more direct electronic detectors, but traditional hygrometers are still common.

Then there's the matter of sunshine and rain. It's easy enough to keep a record of the hours of sunlight manually, but ideally a weather station should be able to run automatically, otherwise it would be very labour intensive to have them scattered across a country. How to keep a record of the Sun's activity without human intervention taxed minds for some time before the development of the Campbell-Stokes sunshine recorder, which uses a glass sphere to focus the rays of the Sun onto a record card that is designed to leave a dark scorch mark without bursting into flames. It's crude but effective.

Rainfall has traditionally been measured using simple devices that collect water over a known area, funnelling it into a measuring container – but the problem with a simple rain collector is that it gives no idea how that rainfall happened over time. All that it is possible to say is how much rain fell since the last time the collector was emptied. The more sophisticated pluviograph uses a collection chamber with a float attached to a recording pen that keeps track of water level on a moving sheet of paper, so that the progress of the rainfall can be measured.

The final essential measure of the weather – pressure – which is crucial for forecasting, is a less obvious aspect of the atmosphere. Pressure measures how much one thing is pressing against something else. It combines the amount of force with which something presses with the area over which it is applied. Historically, it was measured in units of pounds per square inch, though now the unit of pressure is the pascal, which is the number of newtons (the standard unit of force) applied to a square metre. Because pascals are small units, atmospheric pressure is often measured in bars and millibars, where 1 bar is roughly the air pressure at sea level. One bar is 100,000 pascals.

Technically, air pressure is a measure of the force with which gas molecules impact on an area of surface. In a container, the gas molecules are shooting all over the place and apply pressure evenly to all the sides of that container. But the atmosphere is rather different. On top of any piece of the Earth (or, for that matter, your head) there is a huge column of air and the atmospheric pressure is largely due to the weight of that column, pulled down by gravity.

In meteorology, pressure has often traditionally been measured in millimetres of mercury. This reflects the classic design of the barometer, the instrument used to measure the pressure of the air (strictly the 'baro' part of the name comes from the Greek for 'weight', so a barometer measures the weight of the air). The early barometers were made by pouring mercury into a long glass tube with one end sealed. The tube was then tipped upside down into a bath of mercury. The pillar of mercury inside the tube would fall down the tube until the pressure of the air on the mercury bath was enough to support the weight of the column of mercury.

The height of the column rises and falls as the atmospheric pressure changes, hence the measurement of pressure as 'millimetres of mercury' is simply taken by measuring how high a standard column of mercury is. But most household liquid barometers were replaced in the 19th century with 'aneroid barometers' which have as their measurement device a small metal chamber with a vacuum inside it, supported by a spring to stop it collapsing under the air pressure. The size of the chamber is monitored by a lever, which magnifies the effect and displays it on a dial. The mechanism is usually quite stiff, so that the dial can be brought to the latest position by tapping it, displaying the change in pressure.

In a weather station, as well as using mercury barometers for immediate measurement, a form of aneroid

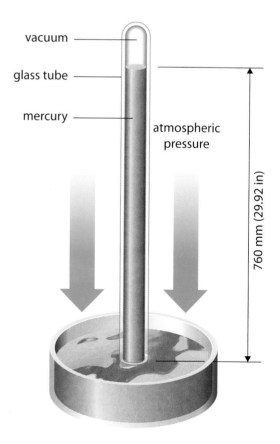

Mercury barometer

vacuum

glass tube

mercury

atmospheric pressure

760 mm (29.92 in)

Aneroid recording
barometer: a barograph

barometer is usually connected to a pen on a slow moving chart, enabling this 'barograph' to keep a constant record of changes in pressure.

Of itself, the air pressure doesn't mean much to anyone other than a meteorologist. Would you know if 1,085 millibars or hectopascals (the same thing) was high or low? In fact it is the highest recorded air pressure – a typical pressure is around 1,015 millibars. But the numbers in isolation have limited value, and what tends to be most important is the relative pressure between two regions, or the changes in pressure in a typical area.

It was observed fairly early on in the history of meteorology that a drop in pressure often indicated bad weather was on the way, giving the barometer an absolutely essential role in weather forecasting. Newton's contemporary (and arch enemy) Robert Hooke, an eminent scientist in his own right, was one of the first to link changes in pressure with the build up of storms and other weather phenomena in the 17th century.

In a region of high pressure, colder air sinks across a region of the Earth's surface (often thousands of kilometres across) and as it comes closer to the ground, this flowing cold air moves outwards, causing a wind that moves away from the centre of the region. Because of the Coriolis effect caused by the rotation of the Earth (of which more in a moment), this flow of air starts to move in a clockwise spiral in the northern hemisphere and anticlockwise in the southern.

Low pressure tends to occur in smaller regions of air over a more compact area. In a region of low pressure, warm air is rising in a column. As it pushes upwards it cools, tending to release rain (hence the association of low pressure with bad weather). As the air moves

Cyclone (low pressure) and anticyclone (high pressure)

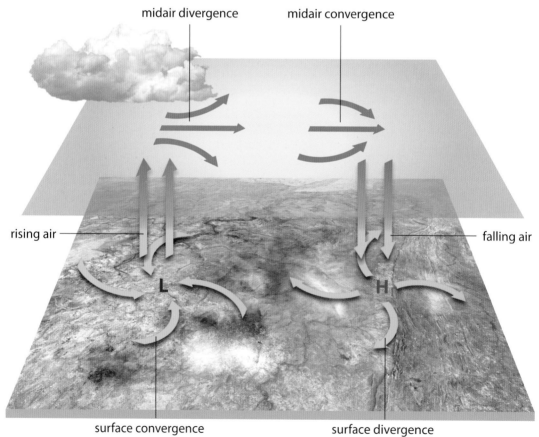

midair divergence   midair convergence

rising air   falling air

surface convergence   surface divergence

Cyclonic flow   **Anticyclonic flow**

into the column at low levels it will spiral round in the opposite direction to a high-pressure region, so in low-pressure regions the air moves in an anticlockwise spiral in the northern hemisphere and clockwise in the south. Because of these spirals, a low-pressure region is sometimes called a cyclone and a high-pressure region an anticyclone.

The Coriolis force reflects the fact that the air is moving on a spinning Earth. If the Earth were stationary, there would be no rotation of columns of low or high pressure, but because of the turning of the Earth, the effect (from our viewpoint on the Earth) is to see the columns of air being twisted in the opposite direction to the way the Earth turns. It has sometimes been suggested that this effect also means water flows down the plughole in different directions north and south of the equator, but in reality the force is only noticeable across something large like a body of air. The direction of circulation of water flowing down the drain is actually influenced by the way the plug is pulled out and by irregularities in the surface it flows over rather than by the Coriolis effect.

By the mid-19th century, the importance of keeping on top of the weather both for travellers and for agriculture resulted in a surge in the development of national weather bureaux. Weather was about to go scientific.

Chapter 2

Weather goes scientific

The increasing use of technology to predict the weather was of great interest to the military. As the art of war was transformed into a science, the impact of weather was inevitably a factor that generals wanted to know about. The Met Office (as the British office for meteorology is universally known) therefore, along with a number of other national weather agencies, was not set up as part of a national scientific establishment, but as an arm of the Ministry of Defence.

This isn't really surprising. Like many other countries, Britain could look back over its military adventures and see how the weather had helped it to victory. Thanks to Shakespeare, Henry V's victory at Agincourt in Northern France, where 6,000 British soldiers defeated a French army of 25,000, has become a great example of the triumph of plucky underdogs inspired to great things by a charismatic leader. But the victory was more down to the weather than Henry's inspirational leadership. Rain turned the battlefield into a muddy mess, bogging down the heavily armoured French fighters and giving the advantage to the lighter weight British archers.

Similarly, when the significantly smaller British fleet faced up to the Spanish Armada in 1588, it seemed likely that invasion would follow. The British had little hope of winning and keeping their independence. Although the outnumbered British ships did do some damage to the enemy, the main force that swung the battle against Spain was the weather. A dramatic storm caught the main section of the Armada, sinking many ships and sending others scuttling for safe harbour.

The establishment of national weather bureaux was boosted by the development of the electric telegraph, which enabled details of weather observations across a wide range of locations to be

Mid-19th century telegraph lines

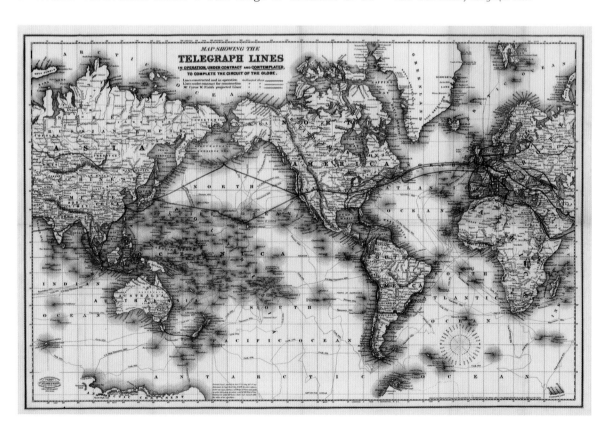

Early TV weather forecast

pulled together to provide an overall picture of conditions, providing a starting point for a forecast.

It isn't always realized just how much of a transformation the telegraph made to society. Before it was invented, the fastest way to get information from place to place was to carry a written message by horseback, or later by train. But the telegraph meant that information could fly across a country at the speed of light. This was the Internet of its day. Suddenly weather information could be gathered from observers across a country and brought together to produce a meaningful picture of the state of the weather nationwide. These weather data were first published in the *Times* newspaper in London in 1861, with the US following 10 years later.

The *Times* also carried the first example of that familiar icon of weather forecasting, the weather chart. Appearing in the newspaper's edition for 1 April 1875, and showing the weather around the UK on the previous day, this visual representation of temperatures and pressures was compiled by the versatile scientist Francis Galton, best remembered now for his ideas on heredity and genetics.

The weather forecast began to catch up with the speed of data collection when it was broadcast over the airwaves with the first ever radio forecast which was transmitted by the UK Met Office on 14 November 1922, but the weather would not be a regular feature of television until November 1947 when forecasts began in Philadelphia. Initially these broadcasts were effectively a radio forecast accompanied by a static picture of a weather map – live human forecasters on the screen, who could manipulate the weather maps, began with the UK Met Office's George Cowling presenting the weather on the BBC in 1954 using weather charts that had been drawn by hand, stacked on an easel.

Weather maps are now generated by computers from data gathered by satellites and other high-tech detection systems, as well as traditional ground stations. There are few other scientific endeavours that have so much raw data to draw on, and that stretches back over such a long period, as has meteorology.

Initially, the sources of information were all ground stations. When governments established weather bureaux, one of the first requirements was to begin collecting data across as wide an area as possible. Ground stations, often staffed by amateurs, would be set up to note basic readings like temperature, pressure, wind speed and rainfall day after day, building up a picture of how a different spread of data resulted in a particular development in the weather. A whole network of local observers spread across a country would be essential for getting a clear picture of regional weather.

Such ground stations are still important, though they are often automated now. Even so, at the time of writing the UK Met Office still makes use of voluntary amateur observers who fill in details from their small local station on a daily basis via a web form (and even, in some circumstances, on paper). This is gradually being replaced by automated systems which collect data via telephone or internet links on an hourly basis, though even with these, some of the readings may have been manually entered by a volunteer, rather than arriving directly from a totally automated system.

Weather balloon

However, what's happening on the ground only gives us a limited picture of the way that weather systems are developing. A lot of the weather takes place further up in the atmosphere. Initially, such operations were carried out by developing small mechanical observatories to be fitted to balloons. Balloons are still widely used, with thousands employed every day around the world to monitor weather developments. They are cheap and easily deployed, though inevitably they are a one-shot approach. In a modern weather balloon, rather than rely on retrieving the balloon and its miniature weather station, results are radioed back automatically.

When aviation (literally) took off in the early years of the 20th century, this was seen as another source of information. Aircraft can penetrate weather systems at altitude with much more accuracy than any balloon. And planes are highly dependent on understanding the weather for safe flying, so it only seemed natural to make use of these flying platforms as mobile weather stations. Even today, with all the other technology available to meteorologists, many commercial flights carry automated weather stations that relay data to the ground, and flight crews often provide direct visual observations, typically every 10 degrees of longitude on the plane's journey, to help build a picture of the prevailing weather.

Important though all these mechanisms are, one technology that wouldn't have entered into the early meteorologists' wildest dreams has now become the mainstay of forecasting – the weather satellite. It was less than three years after Sputnik, the original manmade

Weather satellite TIROS

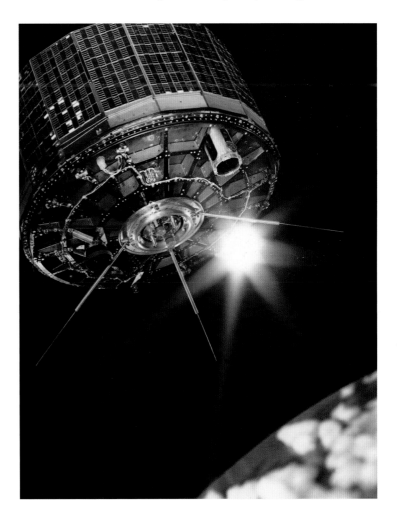

satellite, went into orbit that it was followed by TIROS I, the first of many weather satellites to span the globe.

Since the TIROS launch in April 1960, sending back crude black-and-white TV pictures that enabled forecasters to take a wide over-view of cloud cover, the Earth has been ringed with more and more advanced space technologies analysing our weather systems. As well as high-resolution video, modern satellites capture infra-red images, which enable them to detect the heat emissions from both ground and air, and to capture information at night. Some satellites also add lidar, using lasers in a similar fashion to radar, sending out pulses and watch-ing for reflected photons that are used to detect particles in the air that can reduce light penetration and allow an area below to heat up.

Many of these satellites are geostationary, orbiting 36,000 kilo-metres (22,000 miles) above the Earth's surface. At any particular alti-tude there is a specific speed required to keep a satellite in orbit. In effect what a satellite does is falls towards the Earth under the pull of gravity (there is, after all, nothing holding it up), but at the same time it moves sideways at exactly the right speed to keep missing the Earth. If the satellite travels too slowly it will crash to the ground. If it goes too quickly it will fly off into space. But at just the right speed the two motions cancel out and it ends up staying in an orbit.

At 36,000 kilometres above the Earth, the velocity needed to stay in orbit is exactly the same as the rotational speed of the Earth, so the result is that satellites placed in orbit at this altitude remain over a fixed area and can monitor the same section of the surface as weather conditions change. Other satellites travel around the globe across the poles at a significantly lower height of around 850 kilo-metres (530 miles).

Although weather satellites contribute much of the data that goes into the animated weather maps we now expect to see as part of a forecast, other information comes from a rather older ground-based technology – weather radar. This provides a more localized view than that from a satellite, but it can produce a picture of the intensity of rainfall for around 250 kilometres (150 miles) from the radar source. The radar beams microwaves towards the clouds and the scattered radiation is picked up at the source, indicating both the location and the strength of rainfall patterns.

Weather radar image: Hurricane Hugo

When we see a weather map or hear a forecast, even though they may be aimed at the general public, they tend to be littered with jargon, which it is assumed people will understand. Most us pick up a bit of this jargon by repetition, but some of it remains mysterious. We have already met high and low pressure. Another popular term that forecasters use is a 'front' – usually either a warm front or a cold front. These fronts are particularly interesting to forecasters because they represent boundaries between two masses of air with different temperatures and humidity. Such boundaries tend to bring changes in the weather with them, so meteorologists keep a keen eye on their progress.

A warm front forms when warm, wet air from the tropics enters a region of cooler, drier air. As the warm air moves in, because it is less dense, it slides upwards over the colder air forming a shallow

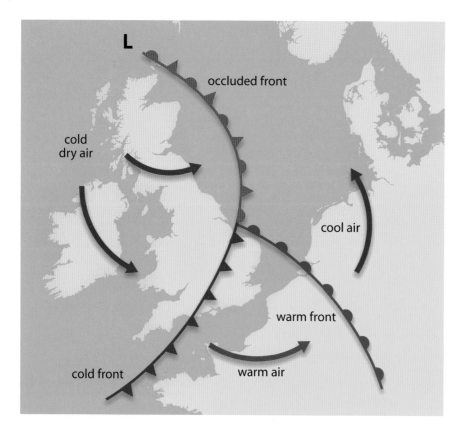

L

occluded front

cold
dry air

cool air

warm front

cold front

warm air

Weather map fronts

sloping boundary between the two. This difference in density – in effect the weight of air in a particular volume – reflects the nature of temperature.

In warmer air, the molecules are moving faster, so they tend to spread out over a larger volume, reducing the density of the air. The region of warm air is pushed up for the same reason a hot air balloon floats in the air or a piece of wood floats on the sea. Because it is less dense than the surrounding material, it experiences buoyancy – the material around it feels a bigger force due to gravity, so the buoyant object (or region of air) floats upwards.

At the boundary between the region of warm air and the cooler air it is moving over, the water vapour in the warm air will cool, often resulting in a prolonged band of rainfall. On weather maps, a warm front is usually represented by a series of semi-circles (red, if the map is coloured) along the line of the front, which is heading in the direction of the symbols.

A cold front is often found close behind a warm front, as cooler, drier air is pushed into a warmer, wetter section. This undercuts the warm air, typically producing a much more concentrated burst of rainfall than a warm front at the boundary, but then clearing the air,

Weather forecasting computers

so that after that heavy shower there often follow blue skies. A cold front is represented on a map as a series of triangles (blue, if coloured) along the line of the front.

A third possibility, less often mentioned but quite frequently seen on the maps, is an occluded front. Here a cold front has caught up with a warm front and undermined it, forcing the warm air further upwards and producing a burst of rain and thick cloud. On a map, warm and cold symbols are alternated along the front line of an occluded front.

For centuries weather forecasting was primarily a manual affair. Data from various stations was collated to produce maps. Outlooks were produced from knowledge of the way different weather systems develop. But now things are very different. Twenty-first century weather forecasting involves throwing vast amounts of data, collected from many different sources, at huge supercomputers that can undertake billions of calculations a second. These computers make use of programs called models, which try to simulate the Earth's climate systems, given the current conditions, and predict how these systems will evolve over the next few hours or days.

Taking a mathematical approach to modeling the climate (as opposed to simply watching for changes in measures like pressure) was first tried by the British mathematician Lewis Fry Richardson, remarkably undertaking repeated complex mathematical manipulations by hand while he was a member of an ambulance crew during the First World War. Richardson's vision, published in a 1922 book, was of thousands of 'computers' – by which he meant human beings undertaking manual calculations – working on data from around the world. The output of these computers would be a prediction of the developing weather. It was an exciting concept, but not practical at the time.

This idea of using repeated calculations to model the climate was revisited in the early days of electronic computers by the mathematician and computing pioneer John von Neumann, who devised the standard architecture for a digital computer. By the mid-1950s, regular modelling of air movements was being undertaken by von

Neumann's team. But it has only been since the 1990s that sophisticated world-spanning computation – the essence of Richardson's visionary concept, though without the army of human calculators – became possible.

Modern computer models that take on the weather do this by breaking the globe up into a set of cells, distorted rectangles (the distortion is because of the curvature of the Earth), each of which is envisaged as having a series of imaginary boxes above it. It's a three-dimensional equivalent of dividing up a flat surface with a grid. The model then works out over time how the current conditions predict things will change from box to box. The smaller and more numerous the boxes, the more accurate is the potential prediction (at least over a short period of time). This is why modern meteorology demands the biggest, most powerful supercomputers.

A huge change happened in the way computerized weather forecasting was undertaken towards the end of the 20th century, which would allow for significantly greater accuracy in forecasts covering 24 hours to five days. The earlier computer forecasts had worked on a single picture of how things were going to be. Forecasters would run the model, and the output would be produced. The problem was that weather systems are so dependent on small changes in initial conditions that any particular forecast was likely to be wrong.

Now, with vastly more computer power, meteorologists will run a model many times, each with subtly different changes reflecting the uncertainties in the data and how the weather will evolve. The European Centre for Medium-Range Weather Forecasting, for example, which supplies such 'ensemble' forecasts around the world, typically runs 50 forecasts per day, each varying slightly in its parameters. The outcomes are grouped together by those with similar results to get a feel for the most likely forecast.

This ensemble approach means that it is possible to get a much better picture of the probability of different weather events occurring, and is why probabilities ('a 40 percent chance of rain', for example) are much more likely to be shown on weather forecasts now. For some reason these are much more popular in the US than the UK, where the forecasters think that the public is not comfortable with probability and needs a firm statement on the upcoming weather.

Nonetheless, a quiet revolution has occurred. Just 30 years ago forecasts were more often wrong than right. Now short-term forecasts are much more reliable. We have become used to this change and still moan when the forecaster gets it wrong – but we have reason for complaint far less often than used to be the case before ensemble forecasts were introduced.

To see why it is so difficult to forecast the weather accurately you need to take a look at the basic physics underlying it. If you go back to Newton's time in the 17th century, there was a new fundamental

Ensemble weather forecast

view of how everything worked that is sometimes called the clock-work universe. The idea was that, given enough data, it is possible to predict exactly what is going to happen, whether you are looking at the paths of comets, the orbits of planets or the vagaries of the weather. However, more recently it has been realized that this is not a realistic picture of the world.

In the broader physical world, we now know that Newton's mechanical picture is too simple. It doesn't correctly match the way in which the particles that make things up, from atoms to photons of light, actually behave. Rather than being totally predictable, the behaviour of these fundamental particles is dependent on probability. What's more, quite often, if we know one particular property in a lot of detail (say, for example, where a particle is), we know less and less about another property (in this case, momentum).

This is Heisenberg's uncertainty principle. This inability to say exactly how each molecule in the air is behaving means that we could never take a particular starting point for the weather systems and predict perfectly, at the level of individual molecules, how things will be at some time in the future. On the whole, though, all the different probabilities average out over the vast number of particles in the atmosphere. Even so, weather forecasting still has a problem with making accurate predictions because of chaos theory.

Chaos theory is a mathematical field developed in second half of the 20th century that has at its heart the idea of a chaotic system. In such a system, a very small change in the way things are at the start results in very large changes as the system evolves through time.

It's no surprise that chaos theory crops up when we are trying to predict the weather. The man behind the theory, Edward Lorenz, was a meteorologist, and it was studying the way small changes in initial conditions of the distribution of temperatures, pressures and winds could make a huge change to a weather forecast that brought him to think about this as a broader mathematical concept.

The most famous application of chaos theory to the weather is actually a myth. This is the so-called butterfly effect. The idea is that if a butterfly flaps its wings on one continent, it starts a chain of events that can result in a storm blowing up half way around the world. (Lorenz was responsible for this concept when he entitled an

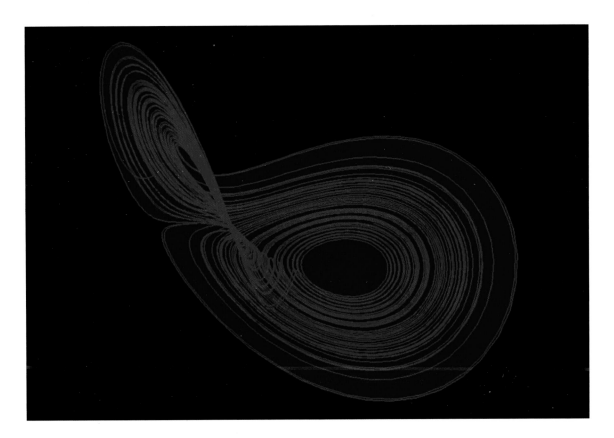

Chaos theory produces 'strange attractors' where a small change in initial conditions can cause a dynamic system like the weather to switch from one mode to another

academic paper: 'Predictability: Does the flap of a butterfly's wings in Brazil set off a tornado in Texas?')

In practice the flap of one pair of insect wings is too small an event compared with the scale of the weather system. The impact it has will quickly be damped and disappear. But the image does dramatically illustrate the point that in the weather a small change to begin with can produce huge differences over time.

What weather forecasters discovered is that if you run a computer model of the weather with slightly different initial conditions – temperatures, pressures and so on – then it does not take long to make huge difference to the way the weather develops. By allowing for this, a combination of excellent satellite observation and modern ensemble forecasting means that forecasts can usually be fairly accurate over 24 hours and have a reasonable stab over three to five days, but anything more than this becomes little more than educated guesswork.

Long-range forecasting remains much more of a dark art than a science, because the potential for change is so great over a longer period. It is certainly true that many long-range forecasts, no matter how much computing power is thrown at them, remain poor. Most of us have encountered promises of a great summer, only to find that the weather is a flop. It almost seems as if long-range forecasts are more likely to be wrong than right.

In part, this failure to predict with any accuracy is because a long-range forecast can only give the broad picture, and local weather can be markedly different from a national average. But it is also nearly impossible to be totally correct when trying to predict a chaotic system like the weather so far into the future. Even so, the quality of long-range forecasting has improved in the last 20 years, in part because we now have a much better understanding of large-scale, long-lasting weather patterns like El Niño (see page 119) which can influence the weather in a large region for a whole season.

A simple way to see how a chaotic system can result in big differences as a result of small changes in starting conditions is by imagining a very narrow mountain range running from north to south. You go up in a helicopter and hover over the range. Move one centimetre to the west and drop a heavy object and it will roll down the mountain to hit the village on the west side. Shift just two centimetres to the east of this razor-sharp ridge and your heavy object will instead roll down the other side of the mountains and arrive in a different village. A couple of centimetres difference in initial conditions makes a huge difference in final outcome (certainly if you live in one of the villages). It's the same with weather.

Forecasting is all about working out what the weather is going to do in a passive fashion. It's about prediction. But it is also possible to manipulate the weather to change what is going to occur in an active way. We do this unconsciously, for example, by pumping carbon dioxide into the atmosphere and increasing the greenhouse effect, or by producing artificial clouds in the form of the long streams of contrails emitted behind aircraft. But weather manipulation is also performed intentionally.

The longest-practised approach to modifying the weather is encouraging rain. Rain may be irritating if all you want to do is enjoy a pleasant day outdoors, but it's essential for growing crops and providing drinking water. Traditionally, cultures have appealed to deities to get a flow of rain going when water has been in short supply. But once it was understood that clouds form when water droplets coalesce on tiny 'seeds' like bacteria or dust, attempts were made to

Cloud seeding

push appropriate seeds into the atmosphere to encourage the formation of clouds and thus improve the chances of rainfall.

The first attempts at seeding clouds used crystals of dry ice – frozen carbon dioxide – which are cold enough (below -70°C) to force water to drop out of vapour form in mid-air. Although this works in principle, there are practical difficulties to using dry ice this way, and more often the seeding material has been silver iodide. This chemical compound is frequently used in photographic materials, as the silver salt darkens when it is exposed to light. Crystals of silver iodide have a similar structure to ice and this makes them particularly good as raindrop seeds. If they are introduced high enough in the sky, where the temperature is already below freezing point but the water is still vapour due to the lack of something to form around, the silver iodide particles encourage the formation of ice crystals that will fall as rain.

At least that's the theory. Although seeding has been carried out since the late 1940s, there is still considerable doubt over the benefit it brings – it is very difficult to measure objectively how much contribution the seeding has made, or whether the rain would have fallen anyway. Even so, cloud seeding attempts continue. In China, for example, silver iodide loaded rockets were used on the outskirts of the Olympic Games in 2008 in an attempt to ensure that the rain fell before it reached the Olympic Stadium, copying an approach traditionally used in the Soviet Union in an attempt to prevent rain from falling on military parades.

Does cloud seeding really work? The jury is still out. But one thing we know for certain is that clouds are an essential (and often beautiful) part of the weather system. So let's head off into the cloudscape.

Chapter 3

Cloud cover

Clouds dominate half our visual span, transforming what would otherwise be a dull, featureless sky into a natural work of art. They provide more dramatic vistas than any landscape, whether you can see the hazy feathering of high cirrus or the dramatic thunderhead of a cumulonimbus. What's more, clouds are the immediate indicator of incoming weather, both bad and good. There are few weather phenomena that don't have some linkage with clouds. Yet most of us know surprisingly little about these floating reservoirs.

At first sight, a cloud seems like the steam that pours from a kettle, which makes it easy to think of it as a gas. But when water is in gaseous form it is transparent – it's invisible. Neither steam nor a cloud is actually water vapour – it's not a gas at all. The visible part is made up of tiny droplets of liquid water suspended in the air (or, if conditions are cold enough, clouds can also be very small ice crystals). It might seem strange that water can just sit up there in a cloud. Why would it float around? If you let go of a drop of water, it falls as quickly to the ground as does a stone. But the droplets in a cloud are much, much smaller. Some are as little as 1/100,000,000th of a metre across, much narrower than a human hair.

This makes these free-floating water drops so small that they are constantly buffeted and bumped by the gas molecules in the air, which zoom around at high speed. The result is that to those water droplets, air seems very thick and difficult to move through, like a ball bearing trying to get through thick treacle. The drops – and hence clouds – do fall, but they sink so slowly that they would only drop by a metre in a year.

Orographic clouds

Another indicator of how fine these water drops are is the sheer insubstantial nature of clouds. They feel practically non-existent to the touch (as you will have experienced when walking through fog, which is just a ground-level cloud) – but they do contain a deceptively large amount of water. Even a reasonably small fluffy cumulus cloud is big enough at around a kilometre across to contain something like 500 tonnes of water.

Clouds come in many shapes, sizes and colours. The shapes of clouds reflect the way in which the water vapour that forms them has risen into the cooler air, where the invisible gas precipitates out as water droplets. Typically, smaller clumpy clouds will be produced by thermals, which are funnels of warm air that rise energetically into the colder air above because the warm air is less dense. This movement of air carries water vapour with it, evaporated primarily from the sea. As the vapour rises into the colder air, it suddenly cools and condenses out as water droplets.

The large clouds that appear to form layers typically reflect the impact of a weather front (see page 39), where a region of warmer air meets an area of cool air, producing a sheet of condensed droplets. There are also some clouds formed by the interaction of moving air with the landscape. 'Orographic' clouds, for example, form when warm moist air moves towards a high ridge. Because the air is pushed up by the rising land, it cools, leaving a string of cloud along the mountain or hilltops.

The range of colour we see in clouds might seem a little odd to begin with. The steam from a kettle is always close to white. We never see black steam pouring from boiling water, yet a thundercloud can look ominously dark. Usually a cloud will look just as white as steam, reflecting a lot of the light that hits it, but when the tiny droplets of a typical white fluffy cloud join together to form the bigger drops that will fall as rain, less light is reflected from the surface of the water, resulting in a darker, grey colour. Snow clouds have a particularly ominous yellow-grey colour that is caused by the ice crystals that will form snow reflecting the incoming sunlight upwards, letting less through.

Droplets in clouds vary between 1/100,000th of a millimetre and 1/40th of a millimetre in size, but by the time they become raindrops

they will have amalgamated with enough of their neighbours to be about 2.5 millimetres across. In practice, clouds never get darker than a shade of grey – they always reflect a fair amount of light – but our eyes tend to exaggerate contrast, and can make them seem almost black when compared with an otherwise bright sky.

As well as the dark grey of a rain cloud, we are also familiar with red clouds, typically near sunset. As we have seen, this effect is caused

Crepuscular rays

by the same phenomenon that makes the sky blue, because blue light is scattered more by air molecules than red. So the sky takes on a blue tint due to this scattered light. But red light has a lower frequency and is less likely to scatter and as the day nears sunset the angle of the Sun to the Earth means that the light needs to pass through more atmospheric particles. This leaves more red light in the illumination from the Sun, and as the fading light passes through more air before it reaches us, so the Sun and any clouds it illuminates seem red.

This lighting effect on the clouds is most dramatic when the Sun has just sunk below the horizon. Because the clouds are higher than the ground, they stay in the sunlight longer – in effect they can see around the horizon by being up in the sky, still basking in the Sun while the land is in the Earth's shade. The result is that the clouds seem to glow above us, still illuminated even though the ground below is no longer getting direct sunlight.

Clouds are also closely associated with another striking visual phenomenon caused by scattered light, which has been given the impressive sounding name, 'crepuscular rays'. These are the visible sunbeams in the sky, dramatic rays where the light is being diffused and scattered by particles and water droplets. They often head downwards, but sometimes upwards, and seem to fan out. We associate them through popular culture with a message from heaven. Downward rays tend to occur through small holes in a cloud (when they are known as Jacob's ladder), while upward rays seem to emerge from the body of the cloud. The fanning out is almost entirely an optical illusion – the rays are close to parallel in practice.

Because clouds have a big impact on the weather they have long been of interest to weather forecasters (as well as to painters and casual onlookers). To make it easier to describe the cloudscape, and hence to assess its potential to affect rainfall and storms, the clouds have long been structured into a scheme that groups them by appearance and height. This cloud typing was started in 1802 by Luke Howard, a London pharmacist with an interest in the weather, but has been made more sophisticated over the years.

Meteorologists now recognize around 52 distinct cloud types, but Howard originally divided them into three families. The clumpy clouds were called 'cumulus' from the Latin for a heap or pile. The layered

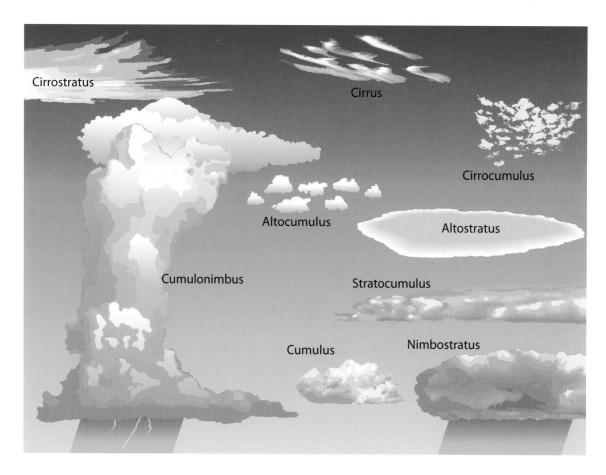

Cirrostratus

Cirrus

Cirrocumulus

Altocumulus

Altostratus

Cumulonimbus

Stratocumulus

Cumulus

Nimbostratus

Cloud types

clouds were 'stratus', meaning a layer or sheet. And the thin, wispy clouds were 'cirrus', taken from the Latin for hair. By 1896, these three categories had been divided into a total of nine basic cloud types, which for convenience were given numbers from one to nine, where nine was the highest on record.

This led to the expression 'being on cloud nine', which indicated that someone was on top of the world – if you were on cloud nine, you were as high as you could get. Unfortunately, as is often the case with scientific scales, the original categories did not prove sufficient to deal with all the clouds as further observations were made. Another category was added, making the highest cloud now cloud ten. Unusually for a scientific body, the World Meteorological Organization had a moment of romanticism and shifted the scale so that it ran from zero to nine, reinstating cloud nine as the cloud on top of the world.

It isn't necessary to go into all 52 types to get a broad grasp of the different cloud forms – we can stick with the basics that cover the vast majority of clouds we are likely to experience. Clouds are categorized by their shape and the height where they typically occur. Coming in lowest is the stratus. This looks rather like a bank of fog, but one that starts above the ground. (Mist and fog are effectively a cloud type that touches the ground, but aren't counted as clouds).

Most stratus clouds form a uniform grey sheet, but some are broken into shreds that drop down from the main body of the cloud, when they become known as stratus fractus. Considerably higher, but still low in cloud terms, comes the children's favourite, the cumulus. These are the ones that look like floating cotton wool blobs, starting

Stratus clouds

Cumulus clouds

around 600 metres up, forming on relatively narrow funnels of rising warm air that are known as thermals.

Another clumpy cloud that can start at the same height, but can also reach much higher, is the cumulonimbus. In fact the highest form of cumulonimbus is the one that provides us with cloud nine, though smaller variants are only cloud three. These are chunky clouds, which in their biggest form, produce a towering anvil shape that can stretch up to 18 kilometres into the atmosphere. Such clouds are sometimes called thunderheads, as they are typically responsible for electrical storms.

The last of the low-level clouds is the stratocumulus. As the name suggests, this is a mix of a layer (stratus) cloud and a blob (cumulus). It can simply be the result of a cumulus that has moved upwards and thinned out into fragments. The most common type of cloud in existence is a stratocumulus that forms a broken layer, sometimes with clear gaps and other times looking more like a high-level stratus that has texturing, rather than being a uniform bank of cloud.

When clouds start a little higher up – typically 1,000 to 2,000 metres – they are given an 'alto' prefix to indicate that they are higher

Cumulonimbus thunderhead

than the base level clouds. So the altostratus is a higher-than-usual stratus. Thicker versions of this usually bring rain and look grey and depressing. When the rain falls, these become a nimbostratus – 'nimbus' meaning that it is a rain cloud.

Cumulus clouds also venture this high as altocumulus, often appearing more like higher versions of stratocumulus than like traditional cumulus, and forming sheets of cover with gaps and fraying, sometimes producing distinct linear bands.

Even higher than the 'alto' clouds, are the truly high-flying clouds, the ones that occur at an aircraft's cruising height (around 6,000 metres or more) and above. Here the air is so cold that those apparently fleecy forms are made almost entirely out of tiny ice crystals rather than drops of water. A common and easily recognizable high form is the cirrus, which forms wispy trails of cloud, often covering a fair amount of the sky.

Both stratus and cumulus types are also represented in the high clouds with the cirrostratus and cirrocumulus. Cirrostratus, as the name suggests, provide more solid cover than the basic cirrus. The cirrocumulus, which can occur up to 14 kilometres above sea level, are topped only by the big cumulonimbus, and sometimes produce a herringbone effect very high in the sky or look like stratocumulus that have ascended too far.

The highest clouds that we see go beyond all the conventional types, forming on the edge of space around 80 kilometres up, where the temperature is as low as -100°C. These are pure ice clouds and are almost invisible during the day. At dusk, however, they benefit from still being in the sunlight when lower clouds are already shaded from the Sun by the curvature of the Earth. In near-black skies, these clouds glow with the light that is still reaching them and are called noctilucent (night glowing) clouds.

Fog, as we have seen, is classified as a different phenomenon from cloud, though there is no good scientific reason for this distinction. Just as a cloud is a collection of water droplets suspended in the air that doesn't touch the ground, fog (and its thinner cousin mist) is a collection of water droplets suspended in the air that does reach the Earth. To be fog, the ground-hugging cloud has to reduce visibility to less than 1,000 metres, which doesn't require it to be very thick.

Cirrus clouds

Fog can arise for a number of reasons. In autumn and winter, the most common form is radiation fog, where clear skies allow the Earth to radiate maximum heat at night, lacking clouds to act as aerial blankets. If the air is humid, this can result in droplets forming as the temperature falls, producing a ground-level cloud.

Other fogs happen more in spring and summer – a typical example would be a sea fog where warm, damp air moves over the cool surface of the water. This same effect (called an advection fog) also occurs in winter as warmer air moves over the surface of snow. And then, of course, there is the confused phenomenon that is hill fog, which is really just a conventional cloud that happens to have run into land that is high enough to reach into its droplets.

Although volcanoes are not themselves a weather phenomenon, being purely geological, they can have a huge influence over the weather by producing a kind of particle fog. Some volcanoes pour clouds of fine ash into the sky. Perhaps the most dramatic example on record was Krakatoa, which spewed out around 20 cubic kilometres of ash and rock in its 1883 eruption.

The Krakatoa ash cloud became suspended in the atmosphere, reducing the amount of sunlight that could get through and warm the Earth. All such clouds have an influence on the weather – in Krakatoa's case the ash reduced global temperatures by over a degree Celsius and disrupted planetary weather systems for several years.

You don't have to go that far back in time, though, to find volcanoes influencing the weather. In 1991 Mount Pinatubo in the Philippines reduced incoming sunlight levels by 10 percent, bringing down global

Radiation fog

Volcanic ash cloud

temperatures by 0.5°C. And in 2010, Icelandic volcano Eyjafjallajökull shut down European aviation for over a week. Though the eruption was not large enough to cause noticeable global cooling, it had a clear effect on European weather patterns.

We might long for blue skies when we're on holiday, but the skies that we experience most, the skies that are red at night or noctilucent, the skies that make us gasp with their beauty or take cover as

rain heads our way, are the cloudy skies. Clouds make the view more interesting and do much more than simply blocking the rays of our next port of call – the Sun.

Chapter 4

The power of the Sun

The Sun is an icon of good weather, the source of the sunshine that we all enjoy. But our local star is much more to the world of weather than simply the means to enable a spot of sunbathing. Apart from the small contributions that are made by the Earth's rotation, it is the Sun that powers *all* our weather systems.

Out of the 400 billion billion megawatts produced by the Sun, a mere 89 billion megawatts arrive at the Earth – yet that is more than 5,000 times the current global energy consumption of the human civilization. The energy from the Sun evaporates water from the sea to provide clouds and rainfall. And it is also responsible for all the movement of air that dominates the weather.

Energy can get from place to place in three ways. Firstly, it can travel as radiation, which is really another word for light. The visible light we can detect with our eyes is just a small part of the whole spectrum of light (or 'electromagnetic radiation' to give it its full

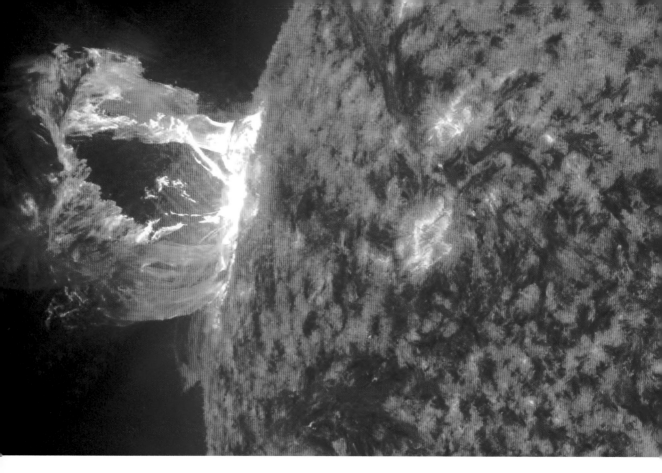

scientific title). Light also encompasses radio, microwaves, infra-red, ultra-violet, X-rays and gamma rays. Visible light apart, the most familiar form of radiant energy is infra-red, because we can detect this particular kind of light with our skin, so we feel heat when infra-red light hits us – but electromagnetic radiation from all parts of the spectrum carries energy.

The second method of transferring energy is conduction. This happens when two physical objects are in contact and energy moves from one to the other. So when you touch a piece of hot metal, the heat is conducted to your fingers and burns you. Conduction is the direct transfer of energy from one object to the other. All particles in an object move around, and a hotter object will have more energetic, faster-moving particles, which bump into the particles of the cooler object and heat it up. It's a bit like billions of tiny car crashes.

Finally, there is energy transfer via convection. This involves the transfer of energy through a fluid, like water, or air. The more energetic, faster-moving molecules travel through the cooler molecules, carrying the heat with them. Warm air is less dense than cooler air, so it rises, buoyed up by the cold air like a boat buoyed up by water. Convection is the main driver of the weather systems within the air itself.

Energy radiating from the Sun

Energy from the Sun crosses the vacuum of space as radiation. It has no choice – neither conduction nor convection can work across empty space because both require a medium. When the Sun's light reaches the Earth, it bombards the molecules of gas in the atmosphere. Each time a photon of light is absorbed by a gas molecule, that molecule gains a bit more energy. As the Sun's light doesn't fall evenly across the whole globe, this means that there will be variations in the amount of energy the Sun gives to the air.

As a result of this, some parts of the atmosphere will become warmer than others. We know why this happens, but the whole system is too complex to be sure exactly what will happen over a broad area simply by observing how the Sun's light falls on the Earth. Whether the air is above sea or land (or snow or trees), the amount of cloud cover, the level of pollution and the area's position on the planet (given that the equator is moving a lot quicker than the poles) will all contribute to the way that the atmosphere warms under the Sun's influence.

The greenhouse effect

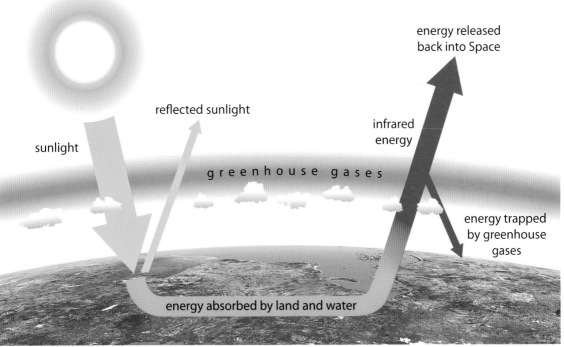

energy released back into Space

reflected sunlight

infrared energy

sunlight

greenhouse gases

energy trapped by greenhouse gases

energy absorbed by land and water

Most of the incoming light will flash straight through the atmosphere and hit the Earth, where it will be absorbed, warming up the ground. Some of the energy doesn't stay there, but is then re-emitted back towards space. This infra-red light, carrying less energy than the visible light from the Sun, heads away from the surface. Some of it is lost into space, but there are molecules in the atmosphere that are good at absorbing this lower energy light and send it flying back towards the Earth again. These gas molecules act as a kind of insulating blanket – they are called greenhouse gases.

With our worries about climate change, we are used to the greenhouse effect being considered as totally negative (See Chapter 12), but in fact the effect is a highly beneficial part of the weather. If it weren't for the greenhouses gases like water vapour, carbon dioxide and methane in the atmosphere, the average temperature on the Earth would be around -18°C, a good 33 degrees lower than it actually is. The greenhouse effect is essential for life – but we just don't want any more of it than we already have.

As the air heats up, its molecules whizz around at an ever-increasing rate. This has a number of effects. A warmed body of air expands, rises and drifts towards the nearest pole. Colder air is pushed out of the way. The result is that air has begun to flow – winds are being created by the localized warming effect of sunlight. As the air moves around, some areas will have relative high pressure, others relatively low pressure, encouraging further movement.

Near the Earth, how much the air moves under the influence of the Sun's rays is limited by friction. The moving air is slowed down by contact with the ground and obstructions like trees and buildings. We tend to see this when objects are moved by the wind – trees swaying in the breeze, or structures damaged by extreme storms – but this friction happens all the time, reducing the energy of the air molecules and slowing them down. Further up in the atmosphere, though, there is no such restraint.

When an area of warm air meets a section of cold air high in the atmosphere, the pressure difference between the two regions can result in a dramatic, high-speed funnel of wind – a jet stream. The bigger the temperature difference between the two regions of air, the higher the wind speed, which is why the most dramatic jet streams (there are four major ones running all year round) occur around the poles. Typically, jet streams are found between 10 and 12 kilometres above the Earth's surface. Rather than simply flowing in a straight line from warm to cold they are deflected, like all large scale winds, by the spin of the Earth as a result of the Coriolis effect (see page 31).

Jet streams

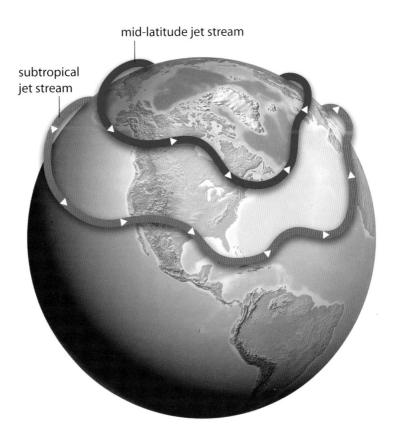

mid-latitude jet stream

subtropical
jet stream

Jet streams were first noticed by Japanese meteorologist Wasa-buro Ooishi who spotted their influence on weather balloons sent up near Mount Fuji. But the practical impact of these high-speed winds was only discovered in the Second World War when US bombers struggled to lock onto their targets over Tokyo. They had entered the jet stream. Although they were flying at around 650 kilometres per hour with respect to the air, the speed of the wind meant that they were achieving 880 kilometres per hour over the ground.

We now know that the fastest jet streams can travel at up to 450 kilometres per hour and they are regularly used by commercial aviation. When flying across the Atlantic towards Europe, for example, airliners slip into the jet stream to gain extra speed, but avoid it on the return journey, where they would be flying into the wind. Conventional aircraft regularly fly faster than the speed of sound (around 340 metres per second – 1230 kilometres or 760 miles per hour) with respect to the ground when carried along by the jet stream.

The winds are not the limits of the influence of our local star. The Sun also provides the potential energy that will be converted into dramatic lightning storms. And it is responsible for some of the most dramatic visual weather effects from perfect blue skies to rainbows and sundogs. When it comes to weather, it all starts with the Sun.

Just how dramatic the impact of the Sun is can be seen from a weather effect that we tend not to think of as weather at all – the seasons. We know that the Earth travels around the Sun in a near-circular ellipse, but it does so in a tilted fashion. The Earth's axis, the

The Earth's axial tilt produces the seasons

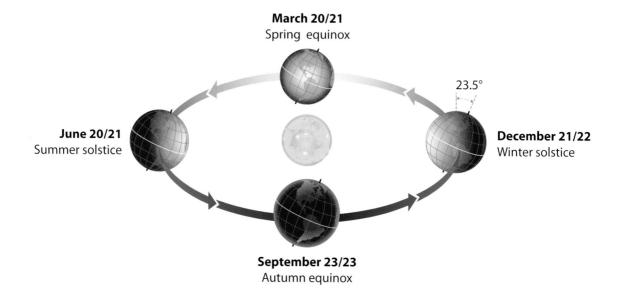

March 20/21
Spring equinox

23.5°

June 20/21
Summer solstice

December 21/22
Winter solstice

September 23/23
Autumn equinox

imaginary line that it spins around, is at an angle of around 23.5° to the vertical, compared with the plane in which it moves around the Sun. This tilt means that for a portion of the year the northern part of the Earth is pointing towards the Sun and for the rest of the year the southern part of the Earth is oriented more in the sunward direction.

This small difference in orientation alters the incoming sunlight and produces the seasons. For half the year the Sun's light and energy hits the Northern hemisphere more directly and for the other half it favours the south. This is the reason that December, for example, is mid-winter in Europe but mid-summer in Australia. In the northern summer, when the northern part of the Earth is tilted towards the Sun, the sunlight has slightly less far to travel and has less air to get through before it hits the ground, when compared with the northern winter.

This small tilt is enough to produce most of the differences in weather between the height of summer and the depths of winter. It is most obvious at the poles, which only receive direct sunlight for half the year. So, for instance, the North Pole only sees the Sun between 21 March and 23 September. For anyone stationed there, the Sun is below the horizon for the rest of the year in a six-month stretch of twilight and night.

Inevitably, a lot of the Sun's energy is absorbed by the oceans. This is hardly surprising when you consider that over 70 percent of the Earth's surface is covered with salt water. Seawater soaks up more of the Sun's energy than the land because it has a higher capacity – which means it takes more heat to warm water than land. Indeed, sand absorbs five times more energy than water.

Because of this, the oceans act as a kind of regulator, heating and cooling more slowly than the land and controlling the temperature cycles of the Earth. They also moderate the absorption of the Sun's energy – energy that keeps us alive and creates our weather.

When sunlight falls on the sea and heats the water, more molecules escape as water vapour. On a large scale, this evaporation is the source of all the water that will produce clouds and, eventually, rainfall.

Chapter 5

Rain, rain

'Rain, rain, go away, come again another day.' We've an ambivalent attitude to rain. We know that it is good for us – there would be no crops and very little drinking water otherwise – yet we don't want it here and now, unless we're in the middle of a heat wave. Rain can also be a weather phenomenon of extremes. Everyday showers are one thing, but a torrential monsoon can wash out a whole town, while flash floods demonstrate the amazing power of even a few inches of fast-flowing water. We might not like rain, but we need to respect it.

Rain has to come from somewhere in a repeated cycle or the skies would run out – and the whole process is dependent on a strange property of water. Water (H_2O) is the only compound that can exist as a gas, a liquid or a solid at the typical temperatures that occur on the Earth. Without this capability we wouldn't experience all the water phenomena that accompany the weather. Water's versatility is possible thanks to a characteristic of the substance that is called hydrogen bonding.

If hydrogen bonding didn't exist, water would boil at below -70°C: It would not exist in liquid form on Earth, and without that there would be no life. Hydrogen bonding is an attraction between the relative

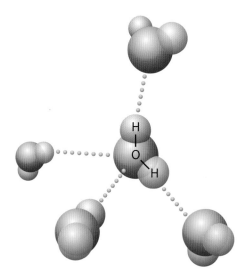

Hydrogen bonding

positive charge on a hydrogen atom in one molecule of water and the relative negative charge on an oxygen atom in another. The result is that the water molecules are harder to separate than they otherwise would be. They stick together, which means it takes more energy – and a higher temperature – to get them to change from liquid to gas. Water gets into the air from liquid water on the Earth – primarily the oceans, but also rivers and lakes – through the process of evaporation. The molecules in liquid water are constantly jiggling about with varying speeds. Those near the surface have more freedom of movement, and the fastest moving molecules can zip off from the surface to become part of the atmosphere as a gas. The warmer the water, the more this will happen. At the same time, some water molecules will rejoin the body of liquid water from the air. The more water there is in the air, the more this will happen.

Water vapour, the gaseous form of water, is a transparent, invisible gas. There are always water molecules in the atmosphere, but we don't see them. However, as water vapour cools when it meets colder air, the water molecules will start to clump together, forming droplets of liquid water in the air. These droplets usually condense on a tiny seed particle – often a bacterium floating in the air.

It's only when the gaseous water in the air becomes liquid (or crystallized as solid ice if it's cold enough) that it becomes visible as clouds, and only when these droplets join together to form big enough drops that it will fall as rain, returning the water to the ground and transferring it from the seas to the land.

Ask anyone to draw a raindrop and the chances are that they will come up with the typical 'teardrop' shape, a streamlined form with the bottom half roughly spherical and the top stretched upwards,

Rain cloud

coming to a point. This simply isn't what raindrops are like. Were it not for air resistance, a raindrop would be spherical, pulled equally in every direction by the surface tension that forms it into a drop. (Surface tension is the work of that hydrogen bonding again – the molecules on the outside of the drop only feel a pull inwards, as there is no hydrogen bonding to pull it outwards. The uniform inward pull naturally forms a sphere.)

In practice the falling drops are buffeted by the air as they fall, resulting in a flattening of the bottom surface – but they certainly aren't teardrop shaped. The reason we think that they are is twofold. The water drops we see most closely are those coming from a dripping tap, and they do take on a teardrop shape as they come close to detaching – but then close up into a sphere as they fall. It's also because when we see falling drops there is an optical illusion caused by the eye taking time to register them, leaving a kind of visual trail that forms the tail of the teardrop.

Rainfall is anything but evenly spread across the planet. Typically the most rainfall occurs around the equator and the tropical regions,

How we think raindrops look

What raindrops really look like

while the driest areas are the subtropical deserts and Antarctica. Surprisingly, this continent of ice and snow, which contains 70 percent of the world's fresh water (which must have fallen from the air at one point) has less precipitation than anywhere else, because the temperature is so low that there is very little water vapour in the atmosphere above it.

This spread of rain around the globe reflects the distribution of high and low pressure in the atmosphere, producing particularly high levels of precipitation where the trade winds come together around the equator. The worst-affected areas shift seasonally with the position of the Sun.

Rain is a general term for a wide range of phenomena, mostly differing in the type of cloud systems producing them. The classic tall cumulonimbus thundercloud produces convective rain, which is the result of the strong updrafts that form those huge clouds, pulling a large amount of moisture up into the heights. This provides the best opportunities for the water to accumulate from the tiny droplets of clouds into sizable raindrops as much as six millimetres across, before gravity overcomes the updrafts and they fall to earth.

The heaviest bursts of rainfall tend to come from these convective processes and from cumulonimbus clouds. This is rain in short, intense bursts – usually lasting less than an hour – with rates of rainfall that can exceed 50mm (2 inches) per hour. The heaviest rainfall in a single day was 1.84 metres/72.4 inches recorded at Cherrapunji in the area of India where tea is grown. The same area holds the records for a month (9.3 metres/366 inches) and a year (26.46 metres/1042 inches in 1860/61) – but the highest long-term measure of rainfall is for Mount Wai'ale'ale on Kaua'i, one of the Hawaiian Islands. This receives an average annual precipitation of 11.68 metres/460 inches.

More prolonged heavy rain tends to come from frontal systems. When a cold front is in charge, it pushes under the warmer air, forcing the warmer air upwards, and causes it to deposit a significant amount of its water content. This type of rain is often responsible for prolonged summer storms, particularly in the western parts of Europe, North America and Australia. These areas are particularly susceptible as they form the meeting point for warm air from the tropics and cold

Monsoon in India

air from the poles. There can also be lighter frontal rainfall at a warm front. In either case, this rainfall from such layered clouds can last several hours.

Even frontal rain is relatively short lived, though, compared with cyclonic rain generated by moist air spiralling into an area of low pressure. Cyclonic rain can fall for days at a time over a large area. Usually, this rainfall will be relatively light. Some will just be drizzle – officially defined as up to 1mm of rainfall an hour – that occurs when the tiny droplets at the base of stratus clouds don't get a chance to accumulate into proper drops, but fall as a kind of descending mist.

A final type of rain familiar to those who live near hills and mountains is orographic rain, where warm, moist air is forced up over the high ground, where it cools and forms cloud. If a rain cloud comes in from over the sea (called a 'seeder cloud') rain from the seeder cloud can fall through the lower cloud that is forming over the hills and drag much of the lower cloud's water content along with it. The result is a particular tendency to perpetual wetness in mountainous coastal regions – the weather in Wales, for example, is often dominated by orographic rain.

A word we now associate with rain, 'monsoon', originally only meant 'season' (it is derived from the Arabic word *mausim*). More accurately, the monsoons are seasonal prevailing winds, which can

OPPOSITE A rainbow

occur in Asia, Africa and Australia, though they are most dramatic in Southeast Asia. The Himalayas are largely responsible for the wetness we associate with the Asian monsoons. These high mountains push up rainfall levels as moist air masses are forced up to unusual heights, causing a lot of the water vapour to condense out. India receives more than three quarters of its annual rainfall during the summer monsoon.

Rain also brings us one of the world's favourite weather phenomena, associated as it is with a mix of rain, clouds and Sun – the rainbow. Rainbows form when strong sunlight shines into a collection of raindrops, hence the need for Sun and rain together. Rainbows appear when the Sun is behind you. Each of the drops of water producing the rainbow acts as a combination of a lens and a mirror to dramatic effect.

When white light from the Sun passes from air to another material like water or glass, the light bends in a process called refraction. White light is made up of the whole spectrum of colours from red to violet, and each colour is bent by a different angle, so the white light

Rainbow formation 1

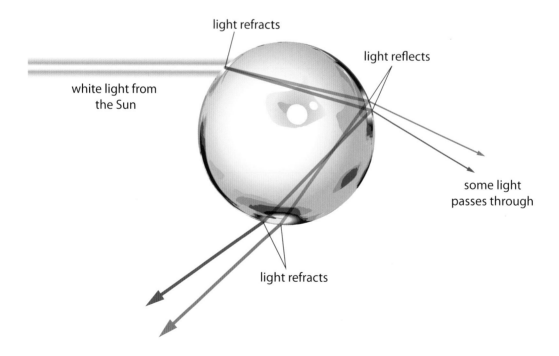

light refracts

light reflects

white light from
the Sun

some light
passes through

light refracts

opens up to form a tiny rainbow. When this multicoloured band hits the back of the raindrop, some of it goes straight through, but some is reflected back, passing through the front of the drop where it is refracted more, and then heads off towards your eye.

If the light is intense enough, some of the photons of light will undergo a double reflection inside the raindrops. This results in a secondary bow, further out than the main one. Because of the second reflection, the colours are reversed from the usual order and the second bow is much fainter.

The rainbow doesn't truly exist out there in the world – it is an optical effect that your eye pulls together from the light emerging from many water droplets – so there is never any chance of reaching the end of the rainbow with its fabled pot of gold (the image always moves ahead of you as you travel). A rainbow is, in effect, a virtual phenomenon, a projection that is no more real than the image on a cinema screen.

Rainbow formation 2

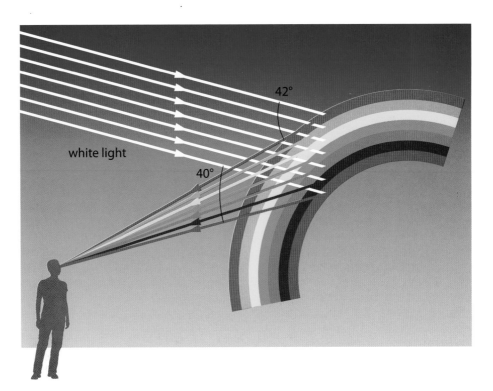

white light

42°

40°

To produce a visible rainbow, the light has to travel in a particular direction. If the angle between the incoming light from the Sun and the light heading for your eye is around 42 degrees you will see a rainbow. The Sun, of course, appears as a circular disc and the rainbow it produces will also be circular, but usually we see the bow as an arc because most of the circle is cut off by the ground. If you are lucky enough to see a rainbow from a plane, with no ground to get in the way, you will be able to see the full circle.

When a full circular rainbow is visible from the ground (perhaps from a mountain top), it produces a subtly different effect called a glory, where a much smaller circle results from the interaction of light hitting raindrops from different directions.

Circular rainbow Oak tree

Brocken spectre

If there are clouds behind a circular rainbow or glory (in the sky or as seen from the ground), then the Sun can cast a shadow of the plane or the person observing it onto the clouds in the middle of the coloured circle. On the ground this is known as a Brocken spectre, as the effect was first spotted from the Brocken in the German Harz mountains, a location that has a strong place in German myth and legend.

Rain may produce beautiful effects like rainbows and glories, and is certainly essential for our survival, but it's unusual for children to look out of the window in the morning and excitedly announce that it's raining. If you freeze that rain, however, you've got a different story.

Chapter 6

The white stuff

Snow and hail may be basically just frozen rain, but the experience of encountering them is totally different. When it starts to rain, we complain, but when big fluffy flakes of snow fall, everyone is thrilled (at least until they have to travel anywhere).

In part it's the sheer beauty of an expanse of pristine whiteness outside your window in the morning before anyone has a chance to set foot in it. Snow might make journeys difficult, but it's hard to argue with its aesthetic qualities. And it's not the only way we can get a stunning white vista – even if there's no snow, frost can transform the landscape into something magical.

Frost is, in effect, what happens to dew when the ambient temperature is too low for the water to stay liquid. Dew most often forms under stable, high-pressure conditions when night-time temperatures fall, turning water vapour into liquid water, seeded by the microscopic bumps and lumps on the edges of plants and other objects. But if

PREVIOUS PAGE Snow

Snow scene

Hoar frost

the surfaces on which the water condenses are below 0°C the result is a hoar frost, forming tiny feathery or needle-shaped ice crystals which grow on vegetation and other cold surfaces. Frost and snow are both crystalline forms of water, and like any other type of ice are transparent – it is air trapped in the structures that causes the familiar whiteness.

A more dramatic form of frost is rime frost, where the moisture in the air is already in the form of droplets as a mist, rather than condensing on the surface directly from vapour. These droplets may already be well below freezing point, but stay liquid in a 'super-cooled' form (water can fall to as low as -30°C without solidifying if there is nothing to seed the crystals) until the water comes into contact with a surface. This triggers freezing, producing a much thicker frost than hoar frost.

Rime frost

If there is a light wind, it will encourage a build-up of rime frost on the side of objects that the wind hits, producing a layer of ice over time that can be several centimetres or inches thick. When this happens on tree branches and fence wire, the result can be a spectacular display of whiteness. This looks impressive, but rime frost also has a downside. It can damage telephone wires with its sheer weight, and can build up on aircraft wings, disrupting the airflow over the wing and making the plane difficult to control, which is why de-icing equipment is an important part of aircraft technology.

It is always cold enough in the high clouds for water to freeze, which might seem to imply that we should always get snow rather than rain – but when temperatures closer to the ground are above freezing, the tendency is for the tiny ice crystals that form in these clouds, which are much smaller than snowflakes, to melt long before they reach the ground. When the air remains cold all the way down, though, these ice crystals can stick together in a process known as aggregation, making larger and larger assemblies of crystals, producing the familiar fluffy flakes.

If the air that the flakes falls through is slightly above freezing point (0°C), flakes will tend to melt around the edges and stick together, forming larger and larger structures until the big fluffy variety are

falling. This contrasts with the powdery snow made up of very small crystals which is more typical when the air is well below freezing point.

The sheer softness of snow before it is compacted is down to the beautiful crystalline flakes, which (unless distorted) are always six sided. This consistent shape reflects the molecular form of water, which consists of an oxygen atom with two hydrogen atoms attached, each at about a 104.5° angle from each other. A combination of this molecular shape and hydrogen bonding (see page 73) means that water naturally forms crystals in a six-sided lattice, and as these molecular scale crystals grow, that six-sided form extends into the exotic six-armed snowflake patterns that are so familiar.

This remarkable six-sided structure was first discovered by the Swedish cleric Olaus Magnus back in 1555, although the full variety of shapes was only made clear with the introduction of microscopes in the early 17th century. Even then, the beauty of snowflakes was not widely appreciated until American meteorologist Wilson Bentley started capturing images of snowflakes with early photographic technology in 1885.

Bentley produced a book of microscope photographs of snowflakes near the end of his life in 1931. This classic work *Snow Crystals*

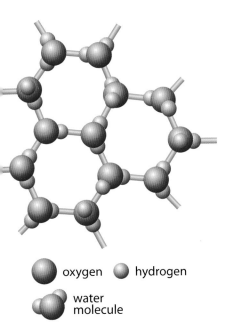

oxygen hydrogen

water
molecule

Ice crystal structure

contained a remarkable 2,000 photographs. It was Bentley who first made the observation, based on his life's work, that 'no two snow-flakes are alike'. There is no scientific foundation for this, and it is easy enough to find identical flakes in the simpler shapes. But it is certainly true that there is a vast variety of snowflake forms.

The traditional delicate snowflake with six arms (called 'dendritic' or tree-like) grows when temperatures are particularly low, while when it is warmer, with the air closer to the freezing point, the snow-flakes tend to form simpler six-sided plate-like crystals. The apparently unique nature of the snowflake shapes is because their growth is governed by chaos, the mathematical concept where very small

Individual snowflakes

changes in initial conditions can result in very large differences (see page 44). Just as this effect makes it difficult to forecast the weather, it also gives immense variety to the way that snowflakes can grow. They are, effectively, fractals, mathematical forms based on chaos.

Near sea level in a temperate region, you will only find snow in the depths of winter, however on the mountains you may see snow even when it's hot and sunny at lower altitudes. If you visit the Alps, for example, it can seem strange to be in a warm, lush Alpine meadow enjoying sunbathing weather while in clear sight all around you the mountains are covered in snow and ice. Given that the vast majority

Range of snowflake shapes

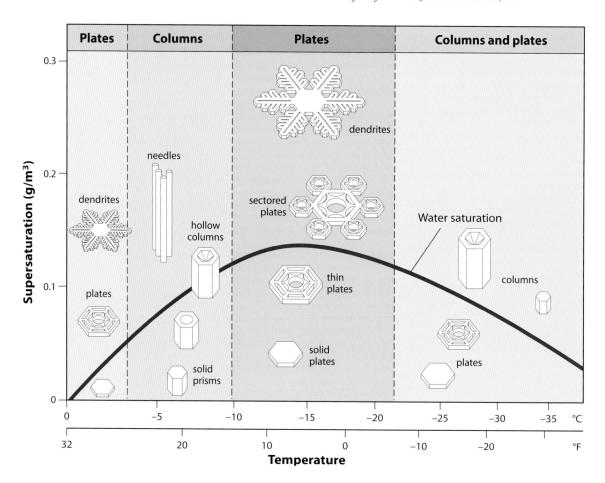

of the heat that keeps us alive comes from the Sun, you might expect that the closer you are to the Sun, the warmer it should be.

It's certainly true that the light reaching us from the Sun is stronger on top of a mountain – so sunblock is essential to deal with all that skin-damaging ultraviolet light – but there is also a thinner atmosphere. Take the train up to the Jungfraujoch railway station – at

Snow on mountain in summer

11,332 feet (3,454 metres) it's the highest in Europe – and already it is noticeably harder to breathe. And, since the atmosphere is thinner, there is less of a blanket to keep us warm. The greenhouse effect is reduced at this altitude.

For roughly every 1,000 metres you climb, the ambient temperature drops by nearly 10 degrees Celsius. So if it's a pleasant 20°C at sea level, by the time you reach 10,000 feet (3,000 metres) you could be experiencing temperatures as low as -10°C. This fall in temperature stops at around 9,000 metres, where there is a different layer in the atmosphere that causes an 'inversion', but for mountain heights, it is going to be chilly enough to keep snow in place all year round.

Greenland ice sheet

Hail storm

When there is snow all through the year, a kind of ice river can form – a glacier. When the temperature is largely below zero but there is also plenty of sunshine, long-term snow melts and refreezes to form a grainy form of ice called firn. This is compacted by any fresh falling snow until it becomes a river of ice. Although solid, this moves under its own weight, lubricated by melted ice between it and the rock beneath, producing a slow-motion flow that moves typically between two and 20 metres a day.

Glaciers can carve dramatic vertical valleys over the millennia (often the presence of these valleys in temperate regions tells a story of a time when ice spread much further over the planet), and these ice rivers carry fresh water down from the mountains. In some areas the ice-cold mountain streams and rivers that form from the glaciers are the main fresh water source for towns and cities, which is why the loss of glaciers due to global warming is so worrying.

Elsewhere – notably at the poles and in Greenland – the glaciers reach the sea without melting, where they spawn enormous icebergs, huge blocks of floating fresh water ice. Icebergs have their own size classifications – some have straightforward descriptions like 'medium' and 'large' but at the small end there are the delightfully named 'growlers' (less than one metre high) and 'bergy bits' (less than four metres high). Famously, the vast majority of an iceberg is below the surface, with often only around 10 percent of its bulk visible – hence the expression 'the tip of the iceberg'.

Snow can transform a landscape to a white wonderland or prove a terrible hazard for travel, but it is generally a much more popular phenomenon than hail. Even in snowy conditions it is possible to get a form of hail that is known as ice pellets. This is when the water crystals freeze together as little grains as they fall, usually coming down in short-lived showers. In the United States such showers are known as sleet, quite different from the British use of the word for a messy, unpleasant mix of snow and rain.

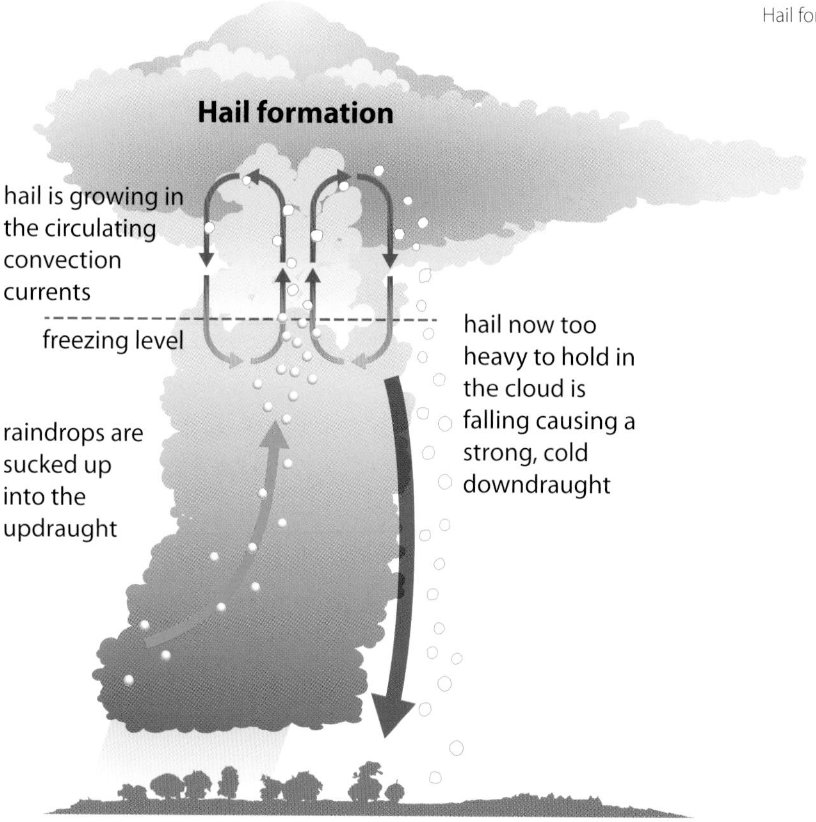

Hail formation

Hail formation

hail is growing in the circulating convection currents

freezing level

raindrops are sucked up into the updraught

hail now too heavy to hold in the cloud is falling causing a strong, cold downdraught

True hail is at its worst in spring and summer. Hail has few positive features above the initial surprise of it starting to fall. It is just irritating – or with hailstones that are bigger than golf balls, positively dangerous. Why are hail and snow so different? Both start as tiny ice crystals. But where snowflakes float down, gradually accumulating extra crystals on their extremities to form their familiar delicate structure, hail has a much more bumpy ride.

Hailstones form in storm clouds. A big cumulonimbus, stretching beyond the altitude at which planes fly, has much more height in which the hailstone can 'grow' than does a typical snow cloud. And rather than simply dropping through the air and accumulating tiny crystals in a fragile form like a snowflake, the hailstones are thrown back up into the cloud by strong updrafts, accumulating more and more layers of ice as they build into solid structures before becoming too heavy to be supported and plummeting to the ground causing irritation or damage.

Large hailstone

The largest hailstones can be 150mm (5.9 inches) across, bigger than a fist. The world record for the weight of a single hailstone is 1 kg (2.2 pounds), which was discovered at Gopalganj in Bangladesh in 1986, while the biggest, found in Nebraska in 2003, was 17.8 centimetres (7 inches) in diameter. The scariest aspect of hailstones is that because they are more massive than any other weather precipitation, and because their terminal velocities can be as high as 140 kilometres per hour (90 miles per hour), they are potentially deadly.

In May 1996 around 100 people were killed in a freak hailstorm in China, which destroyed around 35,000 homes. Hail causes more weather damage in the USA than anything other than tornadoes, accounting for around $1 billion (£637 million/€794 million) of annual losses in agriculture alone. A heavy hailstorm can totally destroy a field of crops or leave a whole street of cars looking as if they have just been through a shooting gallery.

Not surprisingly, we associate snow and ice with cold weather – anything below the freezing point of water (0°C or 32°F) is considered to be seriously cold – but the way we subjectively experience low temperatures is as much influenced by wind as it is by absolute value on a thermometer. With no wind, surprisingly low temperatures seem bearable, but as the wind picks up, wind chill starts to make the experience painful and then deadly.

Wind chill is a problem for two reasons. One is that we tend to use a blanket of warm air as insulation. It's why an animal's fur keeps it warm, trapping air between the hairs. (And why we get goose bumps when we are cold, as our bodies try uselessly to fluff up the fur we no longer have.) It is also why layers of clothes are effective, and why we use fuzzy materials like wool that trap a lot of air. If that air can be kept in place after our body has warmed it up, the air prevents the body from losing as much heat. But a cold wind will disturb that insulating layer, reducing its ability to keep the warmth in.

A second problem is evaporation. It takes energy to make a liquid evaporate, because the attraction between the molecules of the liquid has to be overcome, putting effort into snapping a series of bonds holding it together. The energy to break those bonds has to come from somewhere, and some of it comes from the surrounding

Hail damage

molecules, reducing their kinetic energy. This means they slow down and hence cool down. So when liquid evaporates from a surface, like our skin, we get colder.

This is why we sweat in warm weather. Our bodies are producing liquid on our skin, which can then evaporate and cool us down. This is also why a fan makes us feel cooler when it's hot. Unlike air conditioning, a fan doesn't reduce the temperature of the air; it just pushes it around, causing a wind. The moving air produced by the fan helps increase the evaporation of liquid from our skin, cooling us down.

Similarly, the heat of the Sun doesn't feel so uncomfortable when there's a cool breeze. But it's also much easier to get sunburned if it is breezy because we don't notice the exposure. Burning apart, a breeze is very pleasant when it's hot. But when it's cold, the wind still encourages evaporation, still cools down our skin temperature, even though it's not having any effect on the temperature of the air.

We have always been aware that a wind makes things feel colder, but the real dangers of wind chill were only discovered when explorers headed for the poles and experienced the combination of seriously low temperatures and high winds. It was found that the tendency to suffer frostbite was much more related to the wind speed than it was to the absolute temperature. It is possible to work reasonably effectively in still air at -40°C (-40°F), but throw in even a modest breeze of five kilometres (three miles) per hour and an explorer can get into difficulties.

Wind chill is quantified by trying to indicate the temperature that would be perceived by a human being as a result of adding in the effect of the wind. This is inevitably a subjective process, and the formulae used to calculate wind chill are decidedly messy, involving

Wind chill chart

Temperature (°F)

Wind (mph)	40	35	30	25	20	15	10	5	0	−5	−10	−15	−20	−25	−30	−35	−40	−45
Calm																		
5	36	31	25	19	13	7	1	−5	−11	−16	−22	−28	−34	−40	−46	−52	−57	−63
10	34	27	21	15	9	3	−4	−10	−16	−22	−28	−35	−41	−47	−53	−59	−66	−72
15	32	25	19	13	6	0	−7	−13	−19	−26	−32	−39	−45	−51	−58	−64	−71	−77
20	30	24	17	11	4	−2	−9	−15	−22	−29	−35	−42	−48	−55	−61	−68	−74	−81
25	29	23	16	9	3	−4	−11	−17	−24	−31	−37	−44	−51	−58	−64	−71	−78	−84
30	28	22	15	8	1	−5	−12	−19	−26	−33	−39	−46	−53	−60	−67	−73	−80	−87
35	28	21	14	7	0	−7	−14	−21	−27	−34	−41	−48	−55	−62	−69	−76	−82	−89
40	27	20	13	6	−1	−8	−15	−22	−29	−36	−43	−50	−57	−64	−71	−78	−84	−91
45	26	19	12	5	−2	−9	−16	−23	−30	−37	−44	−51	−58	−65	−72	−79	−86	−93
50	26	19	12	4	−3	−10	−17	−24	−31	−38	−45	−52	−60	−67	−74	−81	−88	−95
55	25	18	11	4	−3	−11	−18	−25	−32	−39	−46	−54	−61	−68	−75	−82	−89	−97
60	25	17	10	3	−4	−11	−19	−26	−33	−40	−48	−55	−62	−69	−76	−84	−91	−98

Frostbite times   30 minutes   10 minutes   5 minutes

Effective 11/01/01

Wind chill (°F) = $35.74 + 0.6215T - 35.75(V^{0.16}) + 0.4275T(V^{0.16})$
Where, T = air temperature (°F)   V = wind speed (mph)

fractional roots of the wind speed, but the result is to be able to say that although the temperature is (say) -10°C (14°F), it feels as if it is -20°C (-4°F) because of the wind. This would happen with wind speeds of around 30 to 35 kilometres per hour (19 to 22 miles per hour).

Despite all the problems of low temperatures, the difficulties snow and ice cause to travel and the risk of wind chill, there is no doubt that snow has the ability to transform the landscape into something beautiful. Frozen rain is weather at its most entrancing. Sometimes, though, weather can be equally striking, but for all the wrong reasons.

Chapter 7

Hurricanes, cyclones and typhoons

Snow is the delicate face of weather, even if it can have immense power when disturbed as an avalanche, but in this chapter we turn to weather in its biggest and most brutal form – hurricanes. At the moment, true hurricanes stick to the tropics (though this may not remain the case if climate change continues). With a minimum speed to be called a hurricane of 120 kilometres (75 miles) per hour, they are immensely powerful storms, which can whip wind speed up to 300 kilometres (186 miles) per hour and wreak havoc when making landfall.

There is a certain amount of confusion over just what a hurricane is, as the term is sometimes used simply to mean a strong

wind. These powerful storms, always arising out at sea, form huge slowly spinning spirals that range from 30 to 40 kilometres (19 to 25 miles) across to an immense 2,000 kilometres (1243 miles) from side to side. They are more typically 500 to 800 kilometres (310 to 497 miles) in width – a massive phenomenon. The spin of a hurricane is usually anti-clockwise in the northern hemisphere and clockwise in the southern, driven by the same Coriolis effect (see page 31) that controls all cyclonic weather patterns.

A hurricane begins as a group of storms in close proximity. If the temperature is at least 26°C and the storms are at least five degrees from the equator, so that the Coriolis force is significant enough to

Hurricane Dennis

pull them into a spiral, the storms can unite as the pressure between the collection of columns of expanding air collapses. The resultant hurricane can be a long-lasting storm, drifting for days or even weeks across the ocean before making landfall, where it will usually disperse in a day or two, but not before potentially causing a huge amount of damage.

It is hurricanes that are responsible for the expression 'the eye of the storm', meaning a sudden lull from dramatic action – and unlike some weather metaphors, this is a real occurrence. As a hurricane passes over, there really is an uncanny still moment at the centre of the high winds and destruction. Seen from above, a well-structured hurricane has a clear gap in the middle. Above the eye, the skies will be clear – this is where the air that is rising around the storm sinks back down. The eye of the hurricane is surrounded by a ring of huge

Eye of hurricane

cumulonimbus clouds, powerful storms called 'hot towers'. This ring is where the winds are most intense and produce the most damage on the ground.

Although hurricanes are obvious on weather satellite images, their paths of destruction are hard to predict as they can suddenly veer off in a new direction, or even double back on themselves. Part of the confusion over just what they are arises from the way that the same phenomenon is given different names in different parts of the world. Though they're probably most familiar as hurricanes in the North Atlantic, Caribbean and parts of the Pacific, exactly the same phenomenon is called a cyclone around the Indian Ocean and a typhoon

Hurricane in 3D

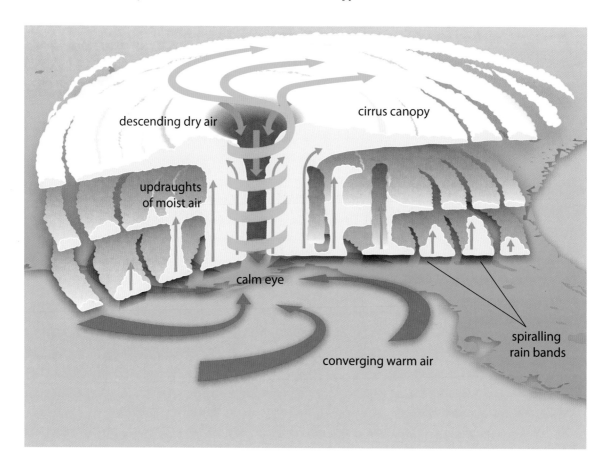

descending dry air

cirrus canopy

updraughts of moist air

calm eye

converging warm air

spiralling rain bands

in the rest of the Pacific and the China Sea. But whatever name they are given, the destruction they leave behind is the same.

The disruption caused by hurricanes has been a constant throughout human history. There might be more devastation in a single event from a tsunami or earthquake, but over time, hurricanes kill more people than any other natural phenomenon. Two attempts to invade Japan by one of the greatest emperors and generals in history, Kublai Khan, were foiled by typhoons. In both 1274 and 1281, the Mongol emperor Khan attempted to add Japan to his recent conquest of China. On both occasions a typhoon blew up and smashed the invading fleet. The grateful Japanese assumed the storm represented protection from the gods. They referred to it as 'kamikaze' – the divine wind.

A more recent example of the deadly power of the hurricane was the devastation produced by Hurricane Katrina in 2005. This left behind a vast swathe of destruction and misery in New Orleans and the surrounding territories. Eighty percent of New Orleans was flattened, leaving 1,500 dead and many thousands homeless. The damage ran to an estimated $81 billion.

Katrina remains fresh in our minds because of the massive media coverage, but far worse was the 1970 cyclone that hit what is now Bangladesh (then East Pakistan). Twenty-foot (six metre) waves were driven up onto the land by the 150 mile-per-hour (241 kilometres per hour) winds, covering 20 percent of the country's land area overnight. Nearly half a million people were killed by this single storm.

As was demonstrated all too horribly in 1970, one of the most devastating impacts of a hurricane is not the wind itself but the storm surge, where the high winds force the sea up to a level that exceeds any normal defences. In part, the sea is simply whipped up higher than usual by the wind – Hurricane Katrina, for example, blasted waves up to 17 metres (56 feet) high, the tallest ever recorded in Louisiana. But there is also a pressure effect.

When a hurricane is travelling over the sea, the low pressure in the spiral of storms around the central eye means that the sea is lifted up – in effect the water around the centre has a greater weight of air pushing down on it, so the water beneath the eye bulges upwards. Out to sea, this effect typically produces a rise of about half a metre

(1.6 feet), although with a big hurricane it can be as much as a metre (just over 3 feet). But when this bulge of water hits land it is concentrated and can result in a surge of more than five metres (16 feet),

Hurricane Katrina

Katrina's storm damage

plenty high enough to cause devastation. The most extreme hurricane storm surges have created 10-metre (33 feet) and higher – the height of a good sized house – pounding onto the coast. Even the less dramatic low-pressure storms that reach the UK cause surges that have made it necessary to build the Thames Barrier in London. This protects the city from inundation by storm surges from the North Sea produced by the pressure effect caused by the eye of the storm.

The storm surge of a hurricane is quite different from a tsunami, which is not a weather effect at all as it is caused by underwater

Tsunami storm surge

seismic activity. In the case of a tsunami (formerly known as tidal waves), an earthquake or an eruption produces a single devastating wall of water that heads for the land.

Hurricanes have their own special scale to give a feel for just how strong they are (the standard wind scale, the Beaufort scale – see page 111 – just has a generic 'hurricane' as its top level). The hurricane scale was developed in the US in the 1960s by structural engineer Herbert Saffir and meteorologist Bob Simpson. The Saffir-Simpson Hurricane Scale accordingly takes account of the building damage likely to be caused. This is generally applied only to Atlantic and Northern Pacific storms. It has five categories as shown in the chart opposite:

Category	Wind speed (kph/mph)	Description
1	119–153 / 74–95	Some damage. Usually causes no significant structural damage but may topple mobile homes and uproot small trees.
2	154–177 / 96–110	Extensive damage. Inflicts damage on doors and windows. Extensive power outages.
3	178–209 / 111–130	Devastating damage. Structural damage to small residences. Flooding near coast destroys small structures.
4	210–249 / 131–155	Catastrophic damage. Some complete roof failures, and extensive building damage. Terrain may be flooded far inland.
5	Over 250 / over 156	Catastrophic damage. Some complete building failures. Collapse of many roofs. Only a few structures capable of surviving flooding.

To make it easier to identify them, hurricanes are given names which can make them sound rather less scary than they actually are. This convention started shortly after the Second World War, initially using the US Army phonetic alphabet (Able, Baker, Charlie, Dog, …) and then changing to women's names, in alphabetical order of arrival during the year. Eventually, a rotating set of four lists was developed, but since the 1970s, when the naming was taken over by the World Meteorological Organization, a series of six lists alternating female and male names has been employed. To make things more confusing, there are different lists and names for around eight different regions of the world, depending on where the hurricane originates, though a storm will usually keep its name even if it moves out of the naming region into a different one.

Although we associate intense storm damage mostly with tropical cyclones like Hurricane Katrina, which require high enough temperatures to keep them in the tropics, there can be powerful storms

The great storm of 1987

at higher latitudes. The usually milder weather of the regions that sit between the tropics and the poles can suffer occasional dramatic features, aptly named bombs. These rare weather events occur when a flow of dry air from the stratosphere brings a sudden plunge in pressure in the centre of an area that is already experiencing low pressure. In a bomb, a huge curl of cloud is usually seen to form a narrow tip like a hook, descending towards the ground, known as a sting jet.

The descending dry air in a bomb appears to evaporate the water droplets and ice particles, which increases the pressure difference in a feedback loop. In Europe, the best-known example of a bomb was the Great Storm of October 1987, which uprooted over 15 million trees in the UK and Northern France. Landscapes were devastated, and pavements were littered with dead birds. Many roads were blocked and buildings damaged. In total, 18 people died. In the US, a bomb in October 1991 produced 30-metre (98 foot) waves in what would become known as 'the perfect storm'.

Hurricanes and bombs are relatively localized, but there are also much larger patterns of air circulation that tend to continue along the same lines year after year, partly because of the rotation of the Earth. The Earth is broadly divided into three sections for each of the hemispheres. There is a circulation at each of the poles, imaginatively known as polar cells, a series of circulatory systems in each of the mid-latitudes known as Ferrel cells after the American scientist William Ferrel, and a series of systems bordering the equator called Hadley cells after the English scientist George Hadley who first described them as far back as the 1750s.

Not all winds, of course, are hurricanes. As we have seen, hurricanes come at the top of the standard wind scale, known as the Beaufort Scale. This often crops up in shipping forecasts, and was originally designed for use at sea (so the definitions of wind speed were originally in nautical miles per hour – knots – rather than kilometres or miles per hour). But the scale is now used widely to give a feel for the impact of wind. Hurricanes top off the scale as force 12. The standardized descriptions of the impact of the different wind levels can be quite poetic:

Beaufort Number	Description	Speed in kph (mph)	Appearance on land	Appearance at sea
0	Calm	0	Smoke rises vertically	Water like a mirror
1	Light air	1–3 (1–2)	Smoke drifts gently	Ripples like scales
2	Light breeze	4–11 (3–7)	Leaves rustle	Small wavelets
3	Gentle breeze	12–19 (8–12)	Twigs move	Large wavelets with scattered white horses
4	Moderate breeze	20–29 (13–18)	Small branches move	Small waves with frequent white horses
5	Fresh wind	30–39 (19–24)	Small trees sway	Moderate waves with many white horses
6	Strong wind	40–50 (25–31)	Umbrellas hard to use	Large waves of 3m (10 feet) with some spray
7	Near gale	51–61 (32–38)	Whole trees sway	Sea heaps up and foam is blown in streaks
8	Gale	62–74 (39–46)	Difficulty in walking	Moderately high waves of more than 5m (18 feet)
9	Severe gale	75–87 (47–54)	Roofs damaged	High waves with toppling crests
10	Storm	88–101 (55–63)	Trees blown down	Sea surface has white appearance
11	Severe storm	102–119 (64–74)	Houses damaged	Waves of more than 11m (38 feet)
12	Hurricane	Over 120 (over 75)	Buildings destroyed	Waves of more than 14m (46 feet)

The scale was extended in 1946 to cover the extent of tropical cyclones, adding forces 13 to 17, but in practice these categories are rarely used today except in Taiwan and some areas of China.

Whether dealing with everyday wind or the most powerful hurricanes, when there is water involved there will be waves. We tend to detach the idea of waves from weather – but they are a weather phenomenon just as much as wind and rain. With the exception of tsunamis, waves are generated by moving air as it flows over the surface of the sea. Wind and waves are closely linked, as demonstrated by the Beaufort Scale.

If you sit by the seaside watching waves crashing on the shore, it seems as if a pile of water is moving towards you, but this is a visual effect that misleads the eye. It is also the reason why a tsunami is so devastating, because in those rare phenomena, a wall of water really is moving towards the shore. But in practice, when ordinary waves arrive they just collapse; they don't deposit heaps of water onto the beach.

Ordinary ocean waves involve water moving in a squashed circle, rotating across the top of the wave, down underneath the sea and back up the other side. The water itself doesn't move forward but cycles around, it is just the wave – the insubstantial shape – that moves onward, leaving the bulk of the water behind it.

Many waves are just ripples in the surface of the water, but the most dramatic ones are the breakers, the white horses, where the blue of the water becomes tipped with a wash of white foam. A wave breaks as it grows higher. As a wave gets taller, the angle of the front of the wave gets steeper, until eventually the top tumbles over, causing the wave to break. In the process, the smooth flow of water becomes turbulent, mixing air into the liquid and turning it into white foam. This happens most often in shallow water, for example near the shore, because there is less room underneath the surface for the water to circulate, thus pushing it higher into the air on top of the water.

It seems reasonable that a storm, with all the power that it carries, can cause devastation, but we forget at our peril that an absence of weather can be equally deadly.

Storm surge North Sea

Chapter 8

Drought

If hurricanes are weather at its most active, there are equal dangers when you could say that there is no weather at all. Take away the winds and clouds, the result is a constant, day-after-day impact of Sun with no rain, which can bring drought and disaster. Whole civilizations have been wiped out by drought, leaving hundreds of square miles of towns and cities, once occupied and thriving, to disintegrate gradually under the merciless Sun. Some of the Earth's most dramatic ruins are the result of evacuation due to drought.

Take the Mayan civilization, which at its height spread across Central America from Mexico to Guatemala. After this powerful culture had been thriving for more than 500 years, it seems to have been cut back suddenly and drastically. Large portions of the southern part of the empire were simply abandoned, leaving behind sophisticated cities with great pyramid structures to be overtaken by the jungle.

All the evidence is that the sudden collapse of this major civilization coincided with a harsh, long-lasting drought. Faced with a lack of rainfall, a population can struggle by for a season, perhaps a year or

Mayan ruins

two. But without massive engineering projects to bring water in from elsewhere, any longer than this and the only possible outcomes are death or evacuation. When the weather no longer provides us with water, life cannot continue.

A more recent episode of abandoning the land occurred in the American Midwest, where a natural drought was made worse by inappropriate use of agriculture. From the mid-19th century onwards, settlers had set up farms on the high plains, ploughing the land. One effect of the ploughing was to disrupt the natural binder of the soil, a plant called shortgrass. In 1930 a drought struck. The topsoil dried out and, without the shortgrass to hold it in place, was blown away, leaving arid and lifeless subsoil. The drought, combined with the mishandling of the ecosystem, rendered mile after mile uninhabitable. In just 10 years over 2.5 million people had to move away from the area.

Drought is very different from most other forms of weather that have a devastating impact on human lives. It is slow and incremental, without the obvious drama of a hurricane, a blizzard or a tornado.

PREVIOUS PAGE Imperial Sand Dunes

Yet there is an inexorable long-term impact that comes with drought. Unlike most weather terms, there is no uniform definition of what a drought is. It's a relative concept that reflects the nature of local climate. In Libya, a drought is two years without rain. In the UK, it is declared after a dry spell of just 15 days.

It's not that UK civilization is so fragile that it is about to collapse if 15 days pass without rain falling, but that period is long enough to start having a noticeable impact on crops and drinking water supplies in a country with a generally moist climate but limited reservoir capacity.

The drying out of the soil isn't the only environmental impact of hot, dry weather. Over time, vegetation becomes dry as a tinder box, and wildfires often sweep across the landscape leaving devastation in

Cotton plant in American drought

their wake. In 2009, the area around the Australian city of Melbourne was hit by uncontrollable wildfires as temperatures soared to more than 46°C (115°F). Despite all the technological capabilities of an advanced country like Australia, 173 people died and around 2,000 houses were destroyed in just one day.

On a landmass the size of Australia, drought and wildfires crop up at the same time as unusual low temperatures. In 2009, while the southeast was a good 10°C above normal and fires raged, the north was ten degrees below normal after a spell of unusually high rainfall.

Over time, an effective absence of weather in a region can be disastrous. Areas that were once green and lush can become deserts, where wind may later sculpt huge dunes into patterns that are beautiful but sterile.

With drought can also come a unique weather hazard – dust storms. When the land has become very dry, high winds can pick up large quantities of sand or earth particles and produce a blinding and crippling wall of dust. Dust storms, sometimes called 'black blizzards', were common in the US drought of the 1930s, while desert countries

Australian savannah fire

often suffer from sandstorms (known as haboobs in the Middle East) which can send a cloud of blinding, choking material flying across a region.

Drought is usually caused when the prevailing weather conditions change. Often this is the result of a jet stream being diverted, something that occurs when there is a change in pressure distribution. This can produce drought in one part of the world and increased rainfall elsewhere. One such factor is the oft mentioned but rarely explained phenomenon, El Niño (in Spanish, 'the boy'). This is what is known as a pressure see-saw (teeter-totter), where two climate-connected zones experience a regular pattern where pressure rises in one area as it falls in the other, and vice versa.

El Niño (or to give it its proper name, the El Niño Southern Oscillation) is a system that crosses the Pacific Ocean, linking the typical high pressure experienced in the Southeast Pacific with the low

Dust storm in Texas

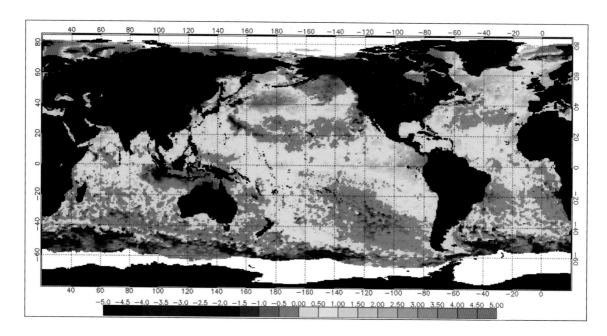

El Niño development

pressure around Indonesia. The result is a regular change in the trade winds blowing across the ocean and a shift in the location of warm water – usually primarily on the Indonesian side – which combine to have potentially dramatic effects on local weather conditions within the affected regions.

As El Niño oscillates, the pressure difference between the South American and Indonesian side of the system varies. As the high pressure weakens, the easterly trade winds across the Pacific drop off and can even reverse. Warm water spreads eastwards from the Indonesian side, heating up the waters on the western coast of South America. This makes it more likely that there will be heavy rain and flooding along the South American coast. The torrential rainfall can cause mudslides that destroy whole villages.

On the Indonesian side, the result is drier than usual weather, risking drought around Australasia, especially in parts of Australia. The prolonged dry spell arising from El Niño also increases the risk of destructive wildfires breaking out. These can be so dramatic that the wildfires in Indonesia during the El Niño events of 1997 and 2006 pumped more carbon dioxide into the atmosphere than is normally produced by the entire planet in a year.

Occasionally the oscillation tips the other way, strengthening the difference in pressures, resulting in cooler water spreading towards Indonesia. Although really this is exactly the same process, just an extreme at one end of the oscillation, it is given the name La Niña (the girl). When La Niña occurs it reverses the typical effects, bringing heavy rain to Indonesia and Australia and dry weather to the South American coast.

This massive weather system does not just influence the countries that fall directly in its path. The extra warm air produced on the eastern end of the system during El Niño rises up and shifts the jet stream that flows from Japan. This tends to bring drier, warmer weather to the northwest side of North America. The shifts in weather patterns can also lead to an increase in rainfall over East Africa, causing flooding

Flooded village, Nigeria

and destroying crops, while West Africa suffers from reduced rainfall and potential drought.

There is an equivalent, although weaker, pressure see-saw falling across the North Atlantic. Known as the North Atlantic Oscillation, this hasn't got a romantic El Niño-style nickname. Instead, its equivalent of El Niño is the less common 'negative phase' of the oscillation, when there is a relatively weak pressure gradient, while the positive phase is more like La Niña, with a strong differential.

The more frequent positive phase of the North Atlantic Oscillation produces the kind of Northern European winters that have been traditionally common, with relatively wet, mild weather over the winter in the North West, but leaving the Mediterranean relatively dry. When the oscillation is in negative phase, Northern Europe tends to be hit by much colder winters, while the more southerly parts are much wetter than usual. Unlike the El Niño system, the effects are felt similarly in both Northern Europe and the East coast of North America.

Systems like El Niño produce flows of sea water as a result of changes in pressure, but they aren't the only way that the oceans contribute to the heating of different parts of the world. A consistent flow of warm water can result in areas that would be frigidly cold without the water flow being pleasantly habitable.

Perhaps the best known of these temperature enhancing sea flows is the Gulf Stream. The name makes it sound like a flowing river, but in fact the process is more like the loop of a conveyor belt. Winds blowing over the North Atlantic cool the already frigid water, which sinks and flows at a low level towards the equator. At the same time water on the surface of the sea is being warmed by the Sun in the Gulf of Mexico – this warm water moves north to compensate for the cold water flowing back far below it.

The Gulf Stream means that northwest Europe is nine degrees Celsius warmer than it otherwise would be – the climate in this region should be more like Siberia. This process, known technically as thermohaline circulation, transports large amounts of heat from the tropics to northern latitudes. It's the collapse of this 'North Atlantic conveyor' that was portrayed so dramatically (and inaccurately) in the movie *The Day After Tomorrow*. The scene as portrayed was not realistic because everything happened much too quickly, and because

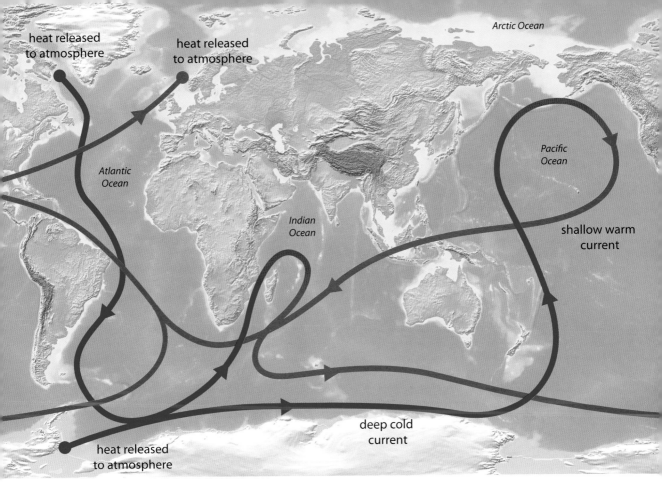

heat released to atmosphere

heat released to atmosphere

Arctic Ocean

Atlantic Ocean

Pacific Ocean

Indian Ocean

shallow warm current

deep cold current

heat released to atmosphere

Global thermohaline circulation

there is no evidence that the conveyor is going to stop at all. But the underlying concept is not entirely fictional.

There is some evidence that a side effect of climate change could slow down the conveyor. This is because more and more fresh water is coming into the oceans from melting ice sheets. This addition decreases the density of the cold water that should be diving down and heading south, as fresh water is less dense than salt water. The result is to reduce the driving force of the conveyor. So in this sense, *The Day After Tomorrow* is not pure fantasy.

Unlike the event in the movie, however, this slowing down is likely to be a very slow process – taking perhaps 100 years to reduce the strength of the Gulf Stream by around 25 percent – a change that will be more than balanced out in its impact by predicted global warming. It could even be a good thing for Europe: such a change would mean that Northwest Europe suffered considerably less from the impact of global warming than other parts of the world.

Thanks to the Gulf Stream, Europe tends to have more of a moderate climate than drought. When it comes to dryness and accompanying lack of rainfall, the world record is held by Quillagua in Chile.

The Day After Tomorrow

Over the 37 years between 1964 and 2001, the average rainfall here was just 0.5mm (0.02 inches) per year. Arica in northern Chile also holds the world record for the longest period without any rain – 173 months from October 1903 to January 1918.

We also tend to associate drought conditions with a dry, arid landscape and a blistering heat. The highest average temperature in the world is to be found in the Danakil Depression which spans northeast Ethiopia and the southern tip of Eritrea, which averages 34.4°C (94°F) across the year. This is an exotic landscape of volcanic activity driven by powerful tectonic movements.

Strangely, the highest temperature ever recorded was in a location that isn't particularly known for prolonged high heat – this was

The Danakil Depression

57.7°C (136°F) at Al'Aziziyah in Libya, south of Tripoli. At the other extreme, the lowest temperature ever measured was -89.2°C (-129°F) in Vostok, Antarctica.

When we consider lack of rainfall it's often associated with heat. The desert is the obvious place for this, but as our cities have become larger, taking away earth and plants to replace them with tarmac and concrete, we have produced a kind of artificial desert. Because of a phenomenon called the urban heat island effect, a city is particularly good at building up heat.

In a natural environment, even in a desert where the heat is unbearably oppressive during the day, temperatures fall rapidly after dusk. Once sunlight is not hitting the ground, the planet loses heat, and with

clear skies this happens rapidly, bringing on the infamous chill of the
desert night. This night-time cooling restricts how high temperatures
can get in the daytime, providing a natural balance.

Vostok Base, Antarctica

In a city, though, there's a problem maintaining this equilibrium.
The pavements, roads and all the surface area of the buildings (particularly if there is a lot of high-rise concrete) act like storage heaters,
absorbing heat during the day and releasing it at night, keeping temperatures artificially high. This is why there were so many casualties
in cities in the European heat wave of 2003. It's the lack of relief from
the heat at night that is the killer. On 12 August 2003, for example,
night-time temperatures in Paris never fell below 25°C (77°F). In a
city where air conditioning is not the norm, this was devastating.

Thousands died from the impact of the heat stored by the city
streets and buildings. In the end, the 2003 death toll was over 35,000
from the heat with another 15,000 from the pollution that built up in
the still air. The US has had even worse overheating problems, though

the prevalence of air conditioning helps mitigate the impact on the human population.

In July 1995, a heat wave struck Chicago. Thanks to the urban heat island effect, on one night the temperature never fell below 27°C

Urban heat island effect in Buffalo, New York

(81°F), while the next it stayed around 29°C (84°F), uncomfortably high for the daytime and impossible to bear at night. Things were even worse in the older tall buildings where the effect of heat rising turned the upper floors into virtual ovens.

The impact of such a pool of heat from a large city can be so significant that it produces its own local weather. There is not just a variation in temperature in the vicinity of the heat island, but the convected heat produces thermals of rising warm air which have been observed to generate winds and storms, complete with thunder and lightning. It's almost as if the weather is fighting back against the city that has distorted its natural patterns.

Thunderstorms like this might be only an irritation, but sometimes a city will suffer from a particularly concentrated storm that can wreak havoc. Even the name raises the hairs on the back of the neck. It's time to meet the tornado.

City thunderstorm

Chapter 9

Tornadoes

Although hurricanes cause more damage than any other kind of storm, they lack the romantic – and visually terrifying – appeal of their distant cousins, tornadoes. These 'twisters' also involve winds that circle at high speed (some tornadoes have been measured with wind speeds of over 600 kilometres/372 miles an hour), but they are very different in scale and structure from hurricanes, typically extending no more than 100 metres (328 feet) across at the base and produced by a different physical process. There are few more graphic images than a tornado in action. This is the most vivid example of the raw force of nature at work.

The conditions required to start a tornado spinning are not what you might expect. Rather than the stormy weather we associate with high winds, the essential ingredient is the heat of the Sun. This warms up the ground, causing thermals – rising pillars of warm air – to form. If the air that is rising is also humid, these thermals will produce fluffy cumulus clouds and, eventually, as the air penetrates further into the atmosphere, the taller and more threatening cumulonimbus clouds form.

LEFT Tornado!

The combination of a strong down blast of air and rain from the cooling cloud coming into contact with the warm air still rising from the ground encourages the spinning effect of the Coriolis force (see page 31) and the whole cloud starts to rotate more and more rapidly. Tornadoes typically form in the late afternoon after the ground has had time to build up heat from the Sun throughout the earlier part of the day to produce a strong updraft.

With powerful enough thermals, the updraft pulls together and narrows. The result is that an initially gentle spin gets faster and faster. This is due to the conservation of angular momentum, just like a spinning skater drawing in her arms and suddenly rotating faster. The spiraling air pulls the cloud down into a funnel shape. When this funnel reaches the ground you have a tornado.

Tornado formation

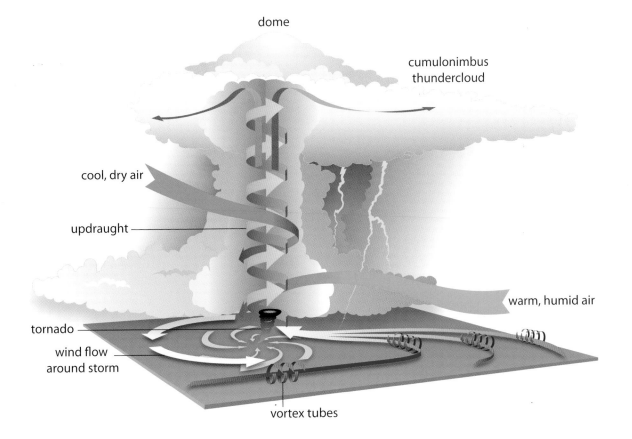

dome

cumulonimbus thundercloud

cool, dry air

updraught

warm, humid air

tornado

wind flow around storm

vortex tubes

Tornado damage

One big difference between a tornado and a hurricane is that while a hurricane blasts objects sideways, a tornado can suck them up into the air, a particularly terrifying prospect as animals, cars, and even parts of buildings are torn from the ground and hurled up in a spinning vortex. The record for surviving being picked up by a tornado is held by a lucky Missouri teenager who was dragged into the air and carried 398 metres (1305 feet) before he fell to Earth. The narrow funnel of fast-spinning air acts like vast vacuum cleaner, sucking up anything it touches. And its random progress over the ground can often seem so spontaneous that it seems to be a living creature.

Although we tend to associate tornadoes with particular parts of the world – states in the US like Texas, Kansas and Oklahoma, for instance – these freak winds can occur anywhere. In fact, the first recorded tornado strike took place in Ireland. On 30 April 1054 the villagers of Rosdalla described a steeple of fire, surrounded at its top by whirling dark birds that picked up animals and pulled an oak tree from the ground. Of course tornadoes have happened for many millions of years before this – it just happens to be the first recorded incident.

Tornado storm

Waterspout

The UK, despite not being known as a major tornado centre, is hit by around 50 tornadoes each year. However, really big twisters require high humidity and a wide area of open land to absorb the heat of the Sun, making the area of the US known as 'tornado alley' (between the Rocky Mountains and the Appalachians) particularly susceptible.

To show just how dramatic the difference is between European and American twisters, where the UK gets around 50 tornadoes a year, in 1999 Oklahoma suffered over 70 tornadoes in a single day, 3 May. In such a large open area, when the conditions are perfect for tornado formation, there is no reason why only one should form. On this particular day, with the ground well heated and humid air funneling in from the Gulf of Mexico, everything was in place for a series of major events. By the end of the day, 40 people were dead and over 2,000 homes had been destroyed, leaving behind a bill for over $1 billion (£640 million/€795 million).

Although most tornadoes occur over land because it generates stable thermals, they can form over the sea, where they are known as sea spouts. When the vortex of air reaches the surface of the sea it sucks up large quantities of water, which will then be dumped back into the ocean when the tornado decays. It's not rising water you see in the waterspout, though: The visible spout is cloud. In the past, many boats have been swamped by these sudden downpours of many tonnes of water.

Because tornadoes require heat, humid air and the formation of clouds, they are often (though not always) associated with thunderstorms. But thunder and lightning are much more widely occurring phenomena. The majority of people have never experienced a tornado, but pretty well everyone has seen a thunderstorm – this is the weather at its most showy.

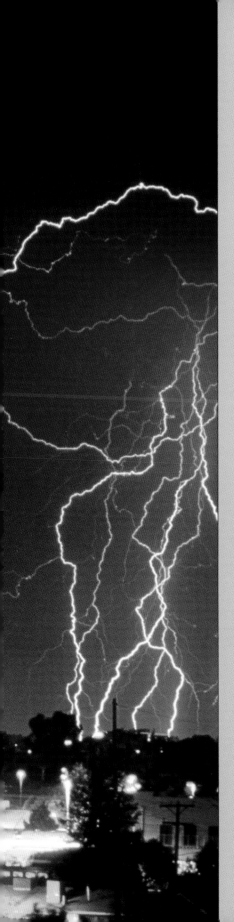

Chapter 10

It's electrifying

Although tornadoes are probably the most iconic weather form in terms of their shape and looks, they have to be seen in daylight to appreciate their full impact. By contrast, the visual fireworks and audible impact of a thunderstorm are most impressive at night. This is weather that cannot be ignored.

In ancient times, thunder and lightning seemed to be a drama being played out on a larger-than-human scale so the phenomenon was usually attributed to the activities of the gods. Often one particular god would be given the role of god of thunder, flinging thunderbolts from the heavens as deadly weapons. The Greeks had Zeus, the Romans an equivalent in Jupiter. The Hindu pantheon is headed up by Indra, while Norse mythology gave us Thor. All of these wielders of thunderbolts were the most powerful gods in their pantheons.

Even if thunderstorms were not directly ascribed to the activity of a divine being, they were thought to be a premonition of bad things to come. Pliny the Elder, writing in the first century AD, considered them to be prophetic, direful and accursed. It's not surprising. A lightning strike could kill, or flash a tree into flames. When a human is hit, it

Thunderstorm

often results in horrific burning and blackening of the skin. There's no doubt that thunderstorms are beautiful – but they are also downright scary. This fear often spreads to animals, which can work themselves into a frenzy during a powerful electrical storm.

Thanks to the old saying that lightning never strikes the same place twice, some rural areas of Britain used to have a brisk trade in what were known as thunderstones. These were stones that had a hole in the middle, which were bought as a safeguard to place up the chimney of a house. The idea was that the thunderstone had already been struck by lighting, which was thought to have caused the hole, so lightning would not hit the chimney, otherwise it broke the 'striking the same place twice' rule.

Thunderstone

Unfortunately, there are two problems with this folk remedy. One is that lightning often does strike the same place twice. If a location is susceptible to lightning strikes it's not unusual to get several hits in one day. The Empire State Building, for instance, has received as many as 15 strikes in a single storm. When you think about it, lightning would have to be conscious and directed if it never returned to the same spot.

Perhaps the most dramatic example of multiple strikes was the US park ranger Roy Sullivan who entered the *Guinness Book of Records* as the person who had been hit by lightning the most times – a total of seven strikes, all of which he survived. The other problem with using thunderstones to ward off lightning is that these unusual formations weren't caused by lightning at all – they are the remains of Stone Age hammers from which the wooden handle and leather binding have long since rotted away.

The English language demonstrates how ignorant we once were about the nature of thunder. It treats thunder and lightning as if they were separate things, which, given that thunder is just the sound produced by lightning, is rather strange. But this reflects the apparent separation of the two effects, because the sounds from a lightning bolt travel a lot more slowly than the light from its flash.

Eiffel Tower struck by lightning

When a ripple of lightning splits the sky, the bolt of light travels towards us at just under 300,000 kilometres per second. By comparison, the noise of that vast bolt of electricity ripping through the air ambles along at 340 metres per second. To all intents and purposes the flash arrives instantly, but you then have to wait for the slow-moving sound to catch up. If a thunderstorm is 10 kilometres (6 miles) away, it will take 29 seconds before you hear the bang.

Basically, lightning is a bolt of electricity. We don't expect electricity to flow through the air because our atmosphere is quite a good insulator. It takes around 30,000 volts to get a spark to jump one centimetre (0.4 inches) in normal humidity. But the damper the air, the easier it is for electricity to flow.

It seems reasonable that dampness helps because we are used to water being a good conductor of electricity (which is why it's not a good idea to get electrical equipment wet). Oddly, though, like air, water is actually a good insulator. Take pure water and it hardly conducts at all. But water almost always contains the ions of substances that are dissolved in it, and these carry the current. Ions (electrically charged atoms) are also responsible for carrying the electricity through the air in lightning, but to produce the vast streams of electric discharge in a bolt of lightning still takes a huge amount of electrical power.

Benjamin Franklin's experiment

It might seem obvious to us, with our wide experience of all things electrical, that lightning has to be some form of electricity, but it is only relatively recently that this was realized. Famously, the American politician and scientist Benjamin Franklin is said to have undertaken an experiment by flying a kite in a thunderstorm in 1752. The kite is supposed to have picked up the electrical charge from the storm which caused a spark to jump from a key that Franklin had attached to the kite string. However, if true, this was extremely risky and could have resulted in his death – kites should never be flown in a thunderstorm.

This experiment has a rather murky history. We don't know for certain that Franklin ever performed it. He certainly proposed trying something like this in a publication issued in 1750, and others undertook it, but there is no reliable documentation of Franklin performing this risky act. If he did, it's unlikely that he flew a kite and waited for it to be struck by lightning, as the legendary experiment is often portrayed. Instead, his proposal was to tap into the electrical charge in the thunderclouds to cause a build up of electricity on a key with no lightning strike taking place. The charge was then to be passed using a wire to a primitive storage device called a Leiden jar, where it could be demonstrated that the power of the storm behaved exactly like ordinary electricity that was generated on the ground.

Considering what a familiar phenomenon lightning is, it's perhaps surprising that we aren't 100 percent certain how the powerful electrical charge is built up. The best-supported theory is that lightning is caused by ice particles and super-cooled water droplets jostling in a cloud, transferring electrons from one to another in the same way a balloon gets an electric charge if you rub it on your hair. In this model, heavier ice particles, typically carrying a negative charge, move towards the bottom of the cloud while lighter positively charged particles are carried upwards. There could also be a connection between the moving particles and the Earth's natural electric field. Either way, the sheer size of a thunderhead or vast cumulonimbus cloud means that the tiny charges add up to produce a vast overall charge.

There is a simple electrical effect that means if you bring a charged object near to another one it will 'induce' the opposite charge in the second object. You can see this in action if you rub a balloon or comb in your hair, which gives it a negative charge (in effect you are rubbing electrons off your hair). If you then bring the charged object near to some small pieces of paper, it induces a positive charge in the nearer parts of the paper fragments because the negative charge on the balloon repels electrons to the opposite side of the paper.

When you carry out this experiment with balloon and paper, the paper is attracted to the induced electrical charge and sticks to the balloon or comb. Similarly, the huge negative charge at the bottom of a cloud induces a positive charge in other clouds or in the ground. (About four out of five lightning strikes go from cloud to cloud, rather than cloud to ground.)

It is this induced charge that can sometimes give warning of a lightning strike. Because a charge is building up on the ground, someone standing near where lightening is about to strike can sometimes feel

Electrical induction with a comb and paper

the build up of electricity, which can make their hair stand on end or produce small sparks. However, such warnings don't always happen, and their absence shouldn't be taken as indicating a safe spot when exposed in a thunderstorm.

Once a significant secondary charge has been induced, something weird happens. There is a relatively weak flow of electricity between the negative storm cloud and its positive target. This flow of electricity ionizes the air. Ions are just electrically charged atoms, which have either had electrons stripped off or added to them – and just as in water, a collection of ions in the air conducts electricity much better than a collection of atoms. This weak discharge from the cloud, called a leader, sets up a path for the main burst of lightning, the return stroke, which goes in the opposite direction – in the case of a ground strike, the main stroke runs from the ground up to the cloud rather than in the obvious direction.

Whether or not Benjamin Franklin took a kite out in a thunderstorm, he certainly did invent the lightning rod (also known as a lightning conductor). The lightning rod was a simple device that consisted of a metal spike on the highest part of a building, connected via a thick metal conductor to the ground. The idea was that this spike was most likely to receive the hit and was intended to conduct the electricity away, reducing damage to the structure. In practice, more often than not the lightning rod prevents a lightning strike from happening in the first place. The rod allows any charge being induced where the spike is located to leak away to the ground, reducing the chances of a leader forming.

When it comes to human beings being struck by lightning, there are a number of simple precautions you can take to reduce the risk of death or injury. Avoid becoming your own lightning rod – get rid of any metal implements like umbrellas or golf clubs and certainly don't hold anything above your head. Get away from high ground and try not to be the highest point around – standing in the

Lightning conductor

middle of an open field on a high ridge is a bad idea. Avoid single trees, which can produce the highest point effect and attract a lightning bolt into your vicinity. Although the tree would initially be struck, there could be enough leakage of electricity to electrocute you too. Also avoid the mouths of caves, which seem to encourage the build up of an induced charge.

Faraday cage

Houses generally make fine places to shelter (ideally staying away from windows and electrical devices) and cars are even better. A metal box like a car, even if it has openings in it, forms something called a Faraday cage. Electrical charges can't get into the cage. The same induction effect that causes a lightning strike means that electrical charges are forced to stay on the outside of the cage because they repel each other. So inside a car you are well protected. Just be careful getting out, as there could be a residual charge on the outside of the car, which could use your body as a conduit to earth if you touch the car and the ground at the same time.

The amount of power in a lightning bolt is phenomenal. To run a 100 watt light bulb for a second takes 100 joules of energy. A single lightning bolt can carry half a billion joules – that's equivalent to the entire output of a good-sized power station run for one second. Many household appliances have fuses that blow if more than three amps of electrical current flows through them. A lightning bolt can easily carry 30,000 amps.

When so much sheer power rages through the air, it blasts the air molecules into frantic activity. The temperature in the vicinity of the bolt of lightning can shoot up to between 20,000 and 30,000 degrees, significantly hotter than the surface of the Sun. As the air expands violently away from the path of the lightning due to this sudden increase in temperature, the result is a shockwave that we hear as the tearing crash of thunder.

Supercell thunderstorm

Thunderstorms most often occur when there is strong surface heating, creating the movement in the air that seems necessary to generate an electrical charge. This means that lightning is much more common over land, and is ideally combined with hot, humid air. The most dramatic thunderstorms happen over tropical and sub-tropical landmasses, with activity dropping off as you head towards the poles.

Thunderstorms are common – there are typically around 1,800 happening around the world at any one time. There can be a huge variety amongst these storms. The most dramatic (and least common) are called 'supercells' which feature a rotating updraft of air feeding a single isolated storm, sometimes producing dramatic circular clouds like something out of a science-fiction movie and also providing the source of tornadoes (see Chapter 9).

Another way that a thunderstorm can be triggered is as a result of a volcanic eruption. This makes for a wonderfully dramatic image as

two cataclysmic forces of nature come together, and lightning plays around the outflow of gases and debris from the volcanic cone.

One contributory factor to a volcanic storm (sometimes called volcanic lightning or a dirty thunderstorm) seems to be the super-heated water vapour that often pours from volcanoes, which can be triggered when a flood of water plunges into a magma chamber. This will instantly and dramatically increase the level of humidity. But it is thought that the main effect may be due to electrical charges building up as the tiny fragments of glass, ash and rock bounce off each other as they fly from the mouth of a volcano, producing a similar process to that of the colliding ice particles building up a charge which is the way we think lightning is formed.

Quite often lightning is seen as a glow in the sky rather than the explicit, forked electrical stroke that is the standard depiction of lightning. This isn't a different phenomenon – it's just that the lightning stroke itself is obscured by cloud, so the result is a diffused glow – but somewhere, above the cloud cover, there will still be a vivid bolt.

There have also been many reports of ball lightning, which usually takes the form of a glowing ball between 20 and 30 centimetres (8 and 12 inches) across that floats through the air quite slowly, with sudden changes of direction and random spurts of activity. These are usually seen during a conventional thunderstorm and have been known to penetrate buildings. When they come into contact with people they tend to disappear, sometimes with a loud noise and burning, but sometimes as if they had no substance at all.

Ball lightning has not been properly studied and there have not been good enough scientific observations of the phenomenon to be sure exactly what is involved, or even if it truly exists at all as a variety of lightning. It is a natural event that is very much at the edge of our scientific understanding, in part because it is so difficult to predict and practically impossible to study in any scientific fashion.

However, there is one ball of energy that we know for certain has a huge influence on our weather. We have already seen how the Sun keeps the Earth at a temperature where life can exist, and generates the weather phenomena of the atmosphere from winds to rain. But the Sun also produces its own form of weather – weather from space.

Chapter 11

Weather from
space

All our normal weather is driven from outer space, powered by light
from the Sun. But there is another kind of weather that comes both
from our local star and the depths of the cosmos. The Earth is constantly bombarded by particles from space. Some are driven from the
Sun in the 'solar wind' while others, cosmic rays, reach us from far
outside the solar system.

The upper atmosphere of the Sun is a constantly roiling mass of
particles, which blasts out streams of electrons (negatively charged)
and protons (positively charged). These flow in all directions, with a
band of them hurtling towards the Earth. Around 1.4 million tonnes
of matter flows out of the Sun this way every second. (If this sounds a
lot, don't worry about the Sun dissolving. It has only lost around 0.01
percent of its mass this way in its 4.5 billion-year lifetime.)

The portion of the solar wind heading off towards the Earth is
the biggest contributor to our direct weather from space. As it nears

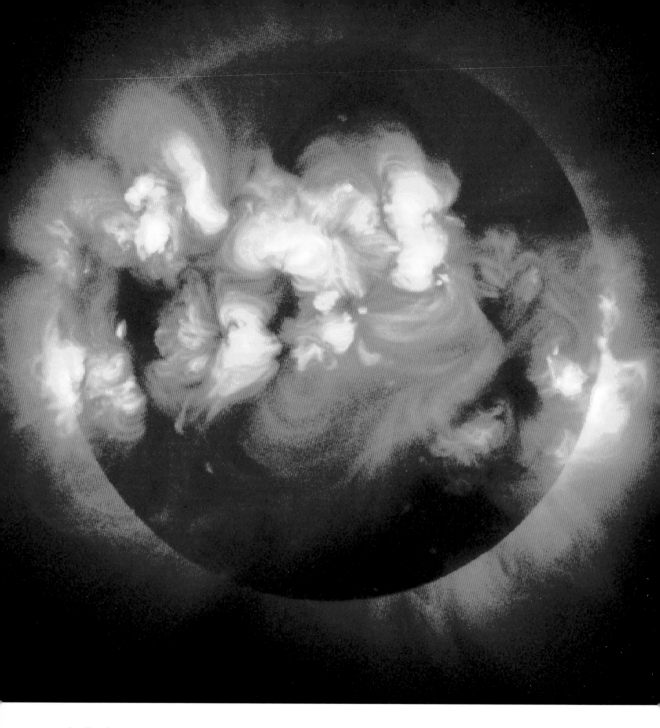

Solar storm

the Earth it comes under the influence of our planet's magnetic field. The Earth is, in effect, a huge magnet, with poles that roughly coincide with the physical north and south pole (which is why we can use a magnetic compass to find direction). In practice, the magnetic poles are around 11 degrees away from the true poles about which the Earth rotates.

The Earth acts as if it had a huge bar magnet through its middle, but the reality of its magnetic power is more complex. Deep below the surface of the planet, the outer core of the Earth is mostly molten iron. This flows around, powered by convection from the hotter inner core. The movement of the liquid metal produces what is, in effect, a huge electromagnet. Moving electrical charges generate magnetism – this is how an electromagnet works, and on a large scale how the magnetic field of the Earth is developed.

When the solar wind encounters the Earth's magnetic field, the magnetism acts as a kind of shield, sending the flow of particles into a detour that forms a roughly spherical shell around the Earth. Without that magnetic field to protect us, we would be constantly bombarded by the solar wind. We can get some feeling for what this involves when we experience a solar storm.

One of these occurred in March 2011. A sudden release of magnetic energy in the Sun's surface formed a solar flare, as if a vast flame had erupted from the surface. This can produce an effect called a 'coronal mass ejection', which blasts out far more charged particles than are usually emitted. A stream of these particles headed towards the Earth at high speed – typically well over 1,000 kilometres (621 miles) per second. As it happened, the 2011 event was relatively minor and passed by without negative effect. But this isn't always the case.

When such a surge in the solar wind, caused by flares and other activity on the Sun, arrives at the Earth, the planet's magnetic field can be distorted in a 'geomagnetic storm'. Because a change in a magnetic field produces electricity (this is how generators work), this can result in stray electrical charges in wiring, disruption of radio (including TV and mobile phones) and other unwanted phenomena, plus dramatic aurora effects which can be seen much nearer the equator than usual.

In principle, the particles of the solar wind can have damaging effects on human beings, rather like the particles emitted from nuclear radiation, but we are well protected by the Earth's magnetic field. Astronauts are far more at risk, particularly when there are powerful flares from the Sun, increasing the high-energy particle flow. A flare in 1989, for example, produced enough high-energy protons so that anyone out in space beyond the Earth's protection (near the Moon, for example) with only a space suit for protection would have been killed.

We are largely protected from the solar wind by the Earth's magnetic field, but some of the influence gets through, creating the amazing visual atmospheric effects of the aurorae, most clearly visible near the magnetic poles of the planet – known as the aurora borealis in the north, and the aurora australis in the south, though there is no difference in the phenomena except for their location.

These remarkable glowing displays in the sky, producing huge shimmering curtains of light, seem all the more dramatic for their pure silence. We are used to the light shows of lightning being accompanied by the roar and rumble of thunder, but the aurorae produce vast sheets and trails that move in stately silence. Usually green, but sometimes stretching into reds and blues, these captivating light shows occur when particles from the solar wind collide with gas molecules in the atmosphere.

A typical reaction contributing to the creation of an aurora would be for a solar wind particle to blast into an oxygen atom. This impact

Solar wind and Earth's magnetic field

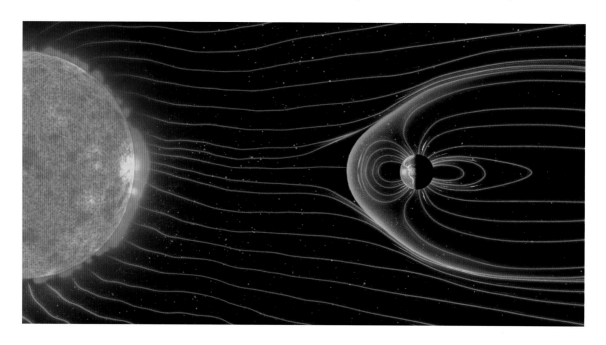

Aurora

gives the atom extra energy, which boosts one of the electrons surrounding the atom into a higher 'excited' state. After a brief moment the electron drops back again to normal levels and in the process gives off the energy it received in the form of a photon of light. The green light generally comes from excited oxygen atoms, while red and blue glows tend to come from nitrogen in the atmosphere.

The reason the aurorae are seen most often and at their strongest near the north and south poles is because the magnetic field of the Earth traps a significant number of the incoming particles in the solar wind and accelerates them towards the poles, so it is here that you are most likely to see these remarkable effects.

Aurorae occur in the vicinity of both poles, though we probably hear more about the aurora borealis, the northern lights. When the Sun is more active than usual, the aurora strays away from the poles towards the equator as the power of the solar wind overcomes the protection of the Earth's magnetic field. This tends to happen when there is a coronal mass ejection, a phenomenon on the Sun that, as we have seen, produces a sudden burst of solar wind.

These bursts of activity are not only associated with solar flares, sudden bright eruptions of activity on the surface of the Sun, but also with sunspots. The spots are apparently dark patches on the 'surface' of the Sun (we have to be a little careful as the Sun is not solid so doesn't have a true surface in the conventional sense). Despite being dark, sunspots indicate a region where there is intense magnetic activity. Although sunspots appear as dark patches, their darkness is only relative. They are typically around 1,000 degrees cooler than the surrounding material, but they are still typically around 3,000°C (5,432°F) and would be brighter than an arc lamp if we could see them in isolation.

Sunspots are a phenomena that were first spotted in China over 2,000 years ago, and with the introduction of telescopes that enabled an image of the Sun to be projected onto a piece of paper, Western

Aurora from space

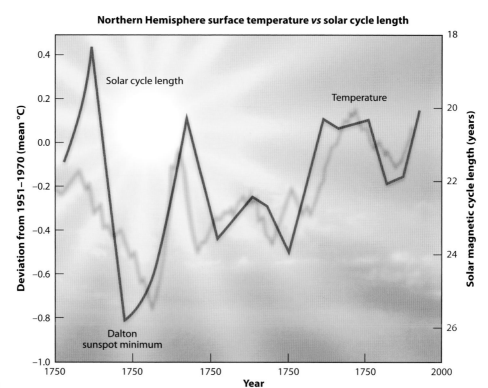

Northern Hemisphere surface temperature *vs* solar cycle length

Link between
sunspots and climate

astronomers have been studying them in detail since the 17th century. It was discovered that the number of sunspots follows roughly an 11-year cycle. There was minimal solar activity around 2008, and the most recent maximum periods of activity were in 2000 and again in 2013.

At times when large numbers of sunspots are seen, there appear to be corresponding increases in solar wind. There also seems to be a link between solar activity and the climate. When large-scale variations in sunspot activity are plotted against temperatures, there does seem, historically, to have been a significant link between the two.

A good example of this variation in climate, which was apparently linked to sunspot activity, was the 'Maunder minimum' a period between 1645 and 1715 when there was an unusually low occurrence of sunspots. Over that same 70 years there was a noticeable change in the climate known as the 'little ice age' when Europe and North America suffered unusually harsh winters with ice fairs held on frozen rivers and many dying from the cold.

The solar weather can also have a dramatic effect on our communications. Ordinary, Earth-bound weather is perfectly capable of disrupting our modern world. Storms or ice can bring down power lines and phone cables, for example. Hot weather has frequently resulted in cables sagging so much that they touch trees and short out, bringing down the power grid. But the Sun is capable of having a much more direct effect.

When the Sun's activity becomes particularly intense, any technology that is dependent on electricity is at risk. The charged particles of the solar wind have the potential to set up electrical currents in wires and to destroy delicate circuits. This became obvious as early as 1859. At the beginning of September that year, a huge solar storm made itself felt on Earth.

With a much heavier than usual impact of solar wind that year, aurorae were spotted as far south as the Caribbean. All of Europe was able to see these dramatic displays in the sky. But the telling impact was on the newly developed electrical telegraph system. The first commercial electrical telegraph had been set up in England in 1839, and 20 years later the technology was already on the way to becoming the Victorian equivalent of the internet. As the storm hit, signalling equipment failed, telegraph operators received electrical shocks, sparks were seen flying from the wires and poles that carried the telegraph signals, and paper on electric telegraph recording devices burst into flames.

This was shocking enough (quite literally) at the time, but if something similar were to occur now, the implications for our electronically dependent world would be truly devastating. Smaller storms since have had a serious impact on radio and TV transmissions, but another storm like the one in 1859 would knock out most of our online world. These storms are thought to occur about every 500 years, but this doesn't necessarily mean it won't happen before then. Although crucial equipment on the ground is protected against the sort of power surges that might happen, many computers and Internet routers would still probably be damaged.

More significantly, a storm on the scale of 1859 would wipe out all our satellites. The impact of a solar storm is much greater in space and the chances of the delicate electronics in satellites surviving the surges produced when the stream of charged particles hit are small. Imagine every satellite having to be replaced. We would lose our GPS

OPPOSITE A cosmic ray with particles

navigation, weather forecasting, and satellite communications for TV, radio, telephones and the Internet.

Although a lot of our communications still use landlines, the capacity for high-speed worldwide communication would be significantly reduced. And replacing every satellite would be both hugely expensive and time consuming. It's hard to imagine we would fully recover in less than 10 years.

When it comes to particles arriving from space, the Sun is our biggest source thanks to its proximity, but the Earth is also constantly bombarded by cosmic rays. These come from deep space, beyond the solar system. The term 'rays' suggests that they are beams of light, but in fact cosmic rays are high-energy charged particles that come crashing into the atmosphere, usually with much higher energy than the solar wind.

Thankfully, many of the cosmic rays that would otherwise hit the Earth are deflected by the same source as the rest of our space weather – the solar wind. As the charged stream of particles that forms the solar wind passes around our planet, ballooning out with the Earth's magnetic field, it acts as a barrier that prevents a fair proportion of cosmic rays from getting through. This means that when the intensity of the solar wind is relatively low, at times of low sunspot activity, significantly more cosmic rays penetrate.

If a cosmic ray particle gets through to the atmosphere it will typically crash into one of the gas molecules in the air. Because it arrives with a huge amount of energy, this results in the production of a shower of particles, emerging from the collision in a kind of inverted firework. For example, an incoming particle might be a positively charged proton. On hitting an air molecule this proton might produce short-lived lighter particles called mesons. These decay to produce both photons of light and other particles called muons. The overall result can be a single incoming particle producing a dozen or more secondary particles, sprouting from its initial collision.

This is the equivalent in nature of what scientists make happen in particle accelerators like the Large Hadron Collider at CERN in Switzerland. Particles are smashed into each other and a whole collection of new particles are formed, partly from the mass of the particles involved in the collision but also from the energy of collision, converting energy into mass according to Einstein's famous equation $E = mc^2$.

Although the muons that are often produced in a cosmic ray shower should decay very quickly and ought not to get far into the atmosphere before they disappear, instead, thanks to special relativity, they often make it to the ground. Special relativity is Einstein's extension of Newton's laws of motion adapted to include the behaviour of light. It shows how objects that are moving experience strange changes. Time slows down for them, they increase in mass and they shrink in the direction of movement.

At everyday speeds the effect of special relativity is not noticeable, but if something is moving at a sizeable fraction of the speed of light, relativity makes a big difference. Although the muons produced by the cosmic rays should disintegrate long before they reach the surface

Cosmic ray shower

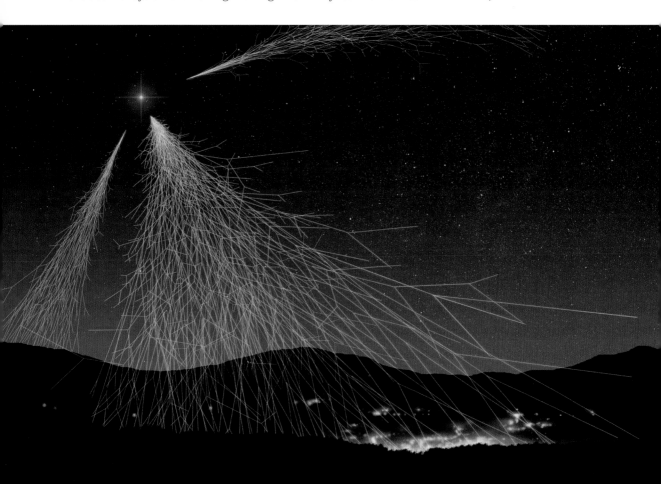

of the Earth, they are travelling so fast that time slows down suffi-ciently for them to survive long enough to be detected. Their lifetime is extended by a factor of five.

There has been some suggestion that cosmic rays influence the weather. In experiments, sending particles like those in cosmic rays through tanks containing water vapour, the particles tend to act as seeds for the vapour to condense producing miniature clouds. It is possible that cosmic rays also influence cloud formation in the real world by the same mechanism.

The impact of clouds on the climate is complex, which is one of the reasons that it is very difficult to predict exactly how the climate will change in the future. We are fairly clear about the impact of clouds on *weather* – at least in terms of rainfall – but how they affect the overall climate, and specifically global warming is more difficult to predict. The broad impact of clouds is that low clouds tend to cool the planet while clouds at high altitudes help warm it by keeping heat in.

It has been suggested that cosmic rays increase the number of low clouds that form, hence cooling the planet. So when the solar wind is relatively light and cosmic rays get through more easily, the sugges-tion is that the density of low-lying clouds will increase, and this is why temperatures tend to fall when there is low sunspot activity. While there is reasonable agreement that this is a contributory factor, it isn't at all certain how big a contribution it makes. Most climate scientists believe that the greenhouse effect, increas-ing as we pump carbon dioxide into the air, has a much bigger impact on the climate than this natural variation driven by the Sun and cosmic rays.

Whatever the exact causes, though, it is impossible to ignore climate change when thinking about our world's weather.

Plotting climate effects

Chapter 12

Challenging the climate

Weather is what we experience directly, but climate gives us the bigger picture and is the overall pattern of weather across time or space. As Mark Twain put it 'Climate is what we expect, weather is what we get.' The difference between climate and weather is why so many people misunderstand climate change. They experience miserable weather (for example cool rainy summers or the unusually cold winters that Europe has experienced in the last few years) and say 'Obviously global warming doesn't exist.'

The reality is that the climate as a whole *is* undergoing change, a change that includes warming when averaged across the planet, but at any one point in space and time we don't experience the average. Because our personal experience is always of the weather not the climate, it is easy to underestimate what the threats of global warming really mean. A temperature rise of a handful of degrees sounds trivial. After all, temperatures vary by tens of degrees between summer and winter. The threats of global warming don't sound dramatic – but that's because they represent an average, reflecting much greater extremes of heat and cold.

Climate change is nothing new. In fact it's perfectly natural. Over the 4.5 billion years that the Earth has existed, the climate has always been in flux, changing many times. Go back to the period with the earliest known life, around 3.7 billion years ago, and things were hot – significantly more so than the direst predictions for climate change – with temperatures around ten degrees higher than they are now.

Between that time and the present, things have also been much colder. There have been four major ice ages in the lifetime of the planet (five, if you count a somewhat lesser one). These are periods when the ice caps extended much further down onto the continents than they do at the moment, transforming the environment in a drastic way. Apart from the damage done by the ice and the difficulty for life to continue in latitudes relatively near to the poles as the ice sheets encroached, the overall global temperatures dropped by around ten degrees below current levels.

Technically we are still in an ice age, the Pliocene-Quaternary, a phase in the Earth's climate that began around 2.5 million years ago. As an ice age progresses, there are periods known as glacials, when the ice is advancing, and interglacials when ice retreats – our current period has been an interglacial for around 11,000 years. During this time (and it's no coincidence that this is the timeframe during which all the great human civilizations have arisen), life on Earth has been relatively easy.

If there were no human interference, the interglacial would be expected to end somewhere between 1,000 and 25,000 years from now, plunging us back into the grip of the ice age. Much of northern Europe, Canada and the northern United States would be hidden under sheets of ice once more. One potential benefit of global warming is that we may already have done enough to stop the next glacial period occurring. (Amongst all the scary headlines we have to remember that warming is not always bad.)

You will sometimes hear those who are concerned for the state of the climate and our human impact on it saying 'We need to save the planet.' This is rubbish. The planet is fine. There is nothing we can throw at it that the Earth can't get over in a million years or two. What we actually want to do is to save our civilization, or at the very least to preserve human existence, which is much more fragile and more affected by changes to the climate than is the Earth itself.

The term we hear most in relation to climate change is the greenhouse effect. As we've seen, of itself this is a good thing, raising the average temperature of the Earth by about 33 degrees from -18°C (0°F) to make it habitable. But we've got enough of a greenhouse effect, and we don't want it to be any stronger. If you want to see the impact of a really bad greenhouse effect, visit our neighbouring

Artist's impression of weather on Venus

planet, Venus. This is quite similar in size to Earth, but has an atmosphere that is 97 percent carbon dioxide (compared with our 0.039 percent). On that runaway greenhouse planet, average temperatures are 480°C (896°F) , and the peak is around 600°C (1112°F).

Climate change is much more complicated than just the greenhouse effect however, which is why there is so much debate about the science. A starting point is that climate change has always happened. As we have seen, during the 4.5 billion years of the Earth's existence the climate has swung between searing heat and icy cold, passing through pretty well every possibility in between. And it has done this a number of times.

Global temperature anomalies

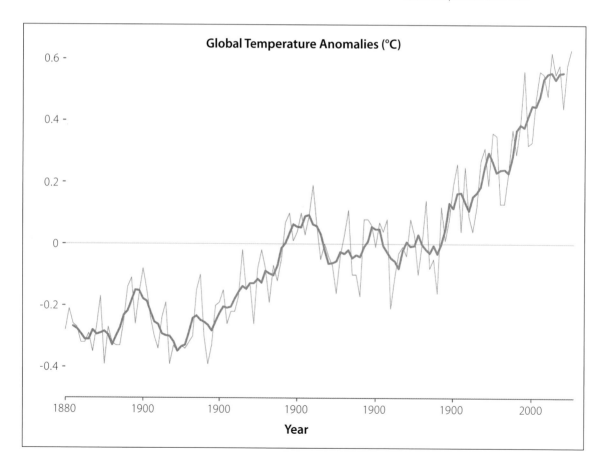

These repeated and vast fluctuations in the climate were clearly not manmade because almost all of them predate human existence. There are plenty of natural causes for climate change. One is the variation in the Sun's output. As well as the sunspot cycle we have already discussed (see page 157), the Sun goes through a number of regular cycles where its output levels rise and fall, plus occasional unpredictable outbursts – and all of these influence climate. Other factors involve the Earth itself. Heavy volcanic activity, for example, can fill the skies with particles that cut down the input from the Sun and drop global temperatures. And, as we have already seen, even cosmic rays from outer space could have an impact on the climate.

However, there is good evidence, which has persuaded the vast majority of scientists around the globe, that human action over the last 150 years is making a significant contribution to climate change. Primarily through increases in the levels of greenhouse gases from industry, homes and transport, we are indubitably having an influence on the climate. And since the 1960s, the rate of global warming has increased. Between 1906 and 2005, global average temperatures rose by less than one degree, but the rise was significantly greater in the second half of the century than it was in the first.

You can see the impact of climate change in what climate scientists rather confusingly call global temperature anomalies. These reflect the way that temperature is measured. It is all very well to ask how the average temperature on the Earth varies, but how do you find out the average temperature of such a huge body, with such varied weather at any one time? It isn't actually possible to calculate a meaningful average for the whole world. Apart from anything else, the spread of weather stations across the Earth's surface is not large enough to achieve this.

Instead, what climate scientists do is use a measurement that isn't an absolute value, but a relative variation, which they call a temperature anomaly. To find the anomalies, they compare average temperatures for any particular period against long-term averages using the same weather stations. This way, any variation in the average temperature (the 'anomaly') sticks out.

This is the main reason why there is some variation in the average temperature comparisons given by different climate monitoring bodies around the world, because the size of the anomaly depends on the period of time used for the comparison, and some have decided to use different periods. This means that they won't necessarily agree on, say, which year was the hottest on record – but they are still all happy to say that the decade up to 2010 was the hottest since records began.

What is much more doubtful is the accuracy of the models predicting just what impact this warming will have on the environment, as there are a huge number of variables, from cloud cover to the melting of ice sheets. The impact of clouds is particularly difficult to model because as we have seen, depending on their altitude, clouds can either increase (high clouds) or decrease (low clouds) global warming, and there is no sensible way to build their contribution into a computer model.

Having said that, the best models are quite effective at predicting the past – when provided with earlier data, they forecast what has happened over the last 100 years reasonably well – and hence have a fair chance of predicting the future. And there is no doubt that warming with a manmade component is occurring. The only disagreement between models is how fast that component is heating things up.

The reason there has been so much debate about the science of climate change is not because of a lack of scientific consensus. There are experts who disagree with specific aspects of climate change prediction just as there are cosmological experts who disagree with the existence of the Big Bang, or physicists who have alternative theories to Einstein's general relativity. Science benefits from the input of those who argue different positions. But we have to go along with the scientific consensus until better data comes along to change this, rather than using the existence of some alternative views as a reason for sticking our heads in the sand. At the moment those who argue against the existence of manmade climate change seem to be doing so for political and business reasons, not because of the science.

Part of the problem with climate change, as we have seen already, is that the basic numbers don't sound too drastic. If we talk about global temperatures rising by a few degrees Celsius or Fahrenheit, so what? Anyone living in a relatively cool climate probably feels that it would be nice if it were a little warmer. We go on holiday to sunny places for a reason. But the detail behind those numbers is more worrying. Much of this arises because of the use of averages, which conceal the existence of peaks, both high and low.

Averages are really useful to get an overview, but they need careful interpretation if we are going to get a feel for what it's really like on the ground. The average person has fewer than two legs (because some people are missing a limb, so the average is below two). Yet the vast majority of people do have two legs. We don't live in an average, we live in specific values, which as far as the weather is concerned means experiencing the peaks and troughs, and just a few degrees of change in the average can make a huge difference to the extremes.

The greenhouse effect certainly influences climate, and we can look back at levels of greenhouse gases in the past by examining bubbles trapped in ancient ice cores, taken from the ice sheets of Greenland and Antarctica. A layer of ice is added to the sheets each year, just like a tree ring, so the further down you drill into the ice, the older the view. These 'cores' are cylinders bored into the ice, which slice through the years, giving a view into the past.

Examining ice cores

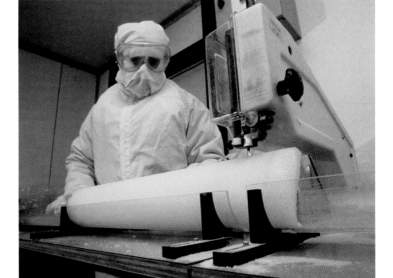

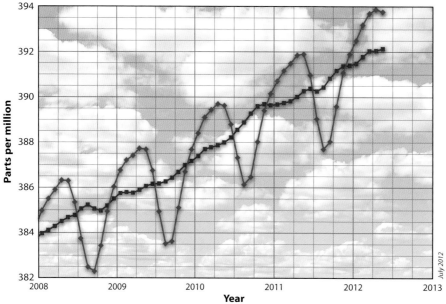

Recent global monthly mean CO$_2$

Parts per million

Year

July 2012

Carbon dioxide levels

From examining the ice cores, it seems that carbon dioxide levels were fairly constant for around 800 years prior to the start of the industrial revolution. Ever since, they have been on the rise and recently the rate of that rise has been accelerating. Pre-industrial levels were around 280 parts per million (ppm) of carbon dioxide, but by 2005 it had reached 380 ppm. If we don't reduce the emissions, it has been predicted that levels could be between 600 and 1,000 ppm by the end of the century.

That's still only 0.1 percent of the atmosphere, which doesn't sound like much, but it is predicted to result, for example, in droughts occurring in the tropics around 13 times more frequently than they do now. It's estimated that in the last quarter of the 21st century, between 1.1 and 3 billion people will suffer from water scarcity. The kind of heat wave that struck Europe in 2003 currently only happens every 20 years or so, but is likely to become annual by the end of the century. And the water that isn't falling as rain doesn't go away. Droughts in some parts of the world are likely to be accompanied by rising sea levels, heavy rains and flooding elsewhere.

Sea level rises tend to be something that the news media like to focus on, because they are dramatic, but strangely they totally miss the main cause of the rise that we are currently experiencing. The images that grab the attention are of vast tracts of ice melting and collapsing into the sea, ice that adds to the water levels of the oceans. But there is very little mention of the basic fact that as water heats up it expands. As there's already a lot of water out there in the oceans, even a small increase in temperature will result in a lot of extra volume. Just a few degrees' increase is enough to raise sea levels by a metre.

The impact of the melting glaciers and climate change is often portrayed by images of isolated polar bears, trapped on ice floes – and there are indeed environmental concerns. But the melting ice surrounding the bears isn't the problem from the point of view of sea level rises. The Arctic, where these polar bears live, is already floating on water—there is no land underneath it. If the ice melts, the sea level doesn't rise, because nothing has been added to the ocean. But while it doesn't add to the sea level, it has effects on wildlife, and because white ice reflects back more light than dark water, the Earth will warm up more quickly if the Arctic ice disappears. But the loss of ice at

Polar bear on ice flow

Antarctic sea cliff

the North Pole doesn't directly influence sea levels. Things are much more worrying, though, in the Antarctic and Greenland.

Both of these feature vast ice shelves that are supported on land. If this ice melts, or sections of it fall into the sea, it has a direct impact on sea levels. Greenland's ice sheet, for example, covers 1.3 million square kilometres (502,000 square miles), and varies between 1.6 and 3.2 kilometres (5,250 to 10,500 feet) in depth. If all the Greenland ice ended up in the sea, the water level would rise by about seven metres (23 feet). In practice, this is unlikely to happen in a hurry. Greenland ice is melting, but it would take thousands of years to completely disappear. But large sheets of the ice can be undermined by melting water and slip into the sea, shifting huge sections of the ice sheet at a time.

There is even more ice in Antarctica. If the fragile West Antarctic ice sheet ended up in the sea, for example, it would push water levels up by about six metres (20 feet). Even a five-metre (16 foot) rise would be enough to swamp many low lying coastal cities like London and New York, not to mention vast swathes of the countryside where land is near sea level. What's more, a one-metre (3 foot) rise can be more than doubled when accompanied by ordinary seasonal storm surges,

Greenland's ice sheet

producing a much higher impact than that metre alone suggests. Over 20 percent of the world's population lives within 30 kilometres (18 miles) of the coast and are susceptible to the impact of a rise in sea level.

Not all manmade climate change produces global warming, though. In fact aerosols have the opposite effect to greenhouse gases. This is not the use of aerosol spray cans, but the impact of fine particles suspended in the atmosphere – soot, for example – which have the effect of cutting down the amount of sunlight that gets through to warm up the Earth, and so causing global cooling. Aerosols produce the same effect as is generated naturally by a volcanic ash cloud, but generally on a smaller scale.

Aerosols and air pollution: Smog in Aviles, Spain

It might seem strange, but even though such aerosols are good for the climate, we have been trying to reduce their presence in the atmosphere for years. This is because these particles are mostly made up of soot, sulphates and other contaminants. They are the kind of particles that create smog and can be extremely bad for the health of anyone breathing them in. Because of this, those building everything from industrial plants to domestic heating and cars have been encouraged to reduce the emission of particles to give us cleaner air. As the big industrial nations continue to improve air quality – in itself a good thing – it does have the side effect of contributing to global warming, as more sunlight then gets through.

Some scientists have suggested we should make use of artificial aerosols, or other large-scale engineering projects that would decrease the sunlight hitting the Earth, or that we should actively reduce the amount of carbon dioxide in the atmosphere in an attempt to get the climate under control. These are interesting, often dramatic schemes. But the problem is that we don't understand the complexities of the climate enough to be sure that our solutions to global warming wouldn't produce a bigger problem elsewhere.

What is clear is that we need to restrain our production of greenhouse gases and be aware of the impact on the environment of everything we do. Climate change is a genuine concern – and the chances are that global warming is going to get significantly worse before things get better – but at least we do now have a much greater awareness of the problems.

Worries about climate change can make it feel as if weather itself is a bad thing, that somehow we would be better off if we could do without it. But we need to remember that weather is equally capable of bringing us beauty, enjoyment and the conditions that make life possible.

Epilogue

The wonder of weather

Weather is something that is always with us, presenting an ever-changing scene, always contributing to our view of the world around us. We might worry about everything that can go wrong with the weather, from climate change to devastating storms, but we ought to remember that without weather there could be no life on Earth – and in this final chapter I want to emphasize the importance of taking the time to enjoy and appreciate all the variety of weather we have met throughout the book.

If you live in a country that has a temperate climate it may seem that the weather is generally rather dull – yet even here it can still surprise you with crystal clear blue skies or the sudden transformation of the landscape brought by a snowfall.

Snow will always have a special place in people's hearts. They may grumble about the inconvenience, but it is a unique part of our lives

(or a sad absence if you live where it never snows). There's something special about the preternatural hush of an undisturbed snow-covered landscape, where everything is just a little quieter that usual – until the children arrive. We often go out and enjoy sitting in the sunshine on a clear day, but snow is more enticing than a mere backdrop. It's the only form of weather where we don't just experience it but directly play with it.

Snowballs and snowmen, skiing and sledging, snow is more than just frozen water; it is a transformation of our landscape that softens contours and changes perspective. It is something we get pleasure from interacting with, whether it's the crunch of snow underfoot or making a snow angel in the garden.

For most of us, snow is a seasonal phenomenon. It may come in the winter, but the majority of the year we live without it. But one weather phenomenon is almost always with us. We certainly appreciate those clear blue skies of summer and the warm Sun that comes with them, but once we've been impressed by the azure backdrop, it lacks excitement. It's a uniform sheet of blue. Skies are much more interesting when they have clouds in them.

All too often we ignore the clouds. And that's a pity. A cloudscape is a natural art gallery. Whether there's a pastoral vista of fluffy white cumulus clouds, a delicate herringbone sky or a looming thunderhead, the clouds are floating sculptures that pass above us. With the colours given them by sunlight and threatening rain, the yellow of a louring storm cloud, the stunning reds of a spectacular sunset, the clouds deserve a few minutes of simply looking and admiring their shapes and hues. It's not for nothing that Ralph Waldo Emerson called the sky 'the ultimate art gallery above'.

We are not just beguiled by the individual shapes of clouds, but by the combinations and interplay of these fantastical forms. When light streams through a gap in the clouds, or a delicate curtain of rain ripples down from the edge of a distant cloud structure, the effects can be breathtaking. Take the time to take another look at the clouds.

One cloud form you won't want to stay out in, though, is a big thunderstorm. Nature's power is evident in the weather and has always inspired fear and awe. But by understanding the science behind it, we no longer see a thunderbolt as the wrath of a god, or think that it

Mammatus cloudscape in Nebraska

will pour for 40 days and 40 nights if it rains on St Swithun's Day. We know that there simply isn't enough water on the Earth to cover the whole surface in a flood like the Biblical story. But that understanding doesn't take away the drama that weather can provide.

When a thunderstorm is underway, we can experience the sheer power of the weather – the scale of it – in all its glory. That there are so many tiny drops of water, each with a ridiculously small electrical charge, joining forces to provide such an awesome display is remarkable. It really puts the size of a thundercloud, a cumulonimbus reaching all the way up to cloud nine, into perspective.

Summer thunderstorm in Tucson, Arizona

What's more, a thunderstorm doesn't just give us the science-fiction drama of those huge electrical discharges, like Frankenstein's laboratory writ large across the sky, it also has its own sound track. Many weather phenomena are silent, or provide a gentle background noise like the patter of falling rain – but thunder is not about to let you ignore it.

Pretty well everywhere in the world experiences regular thunder and lightning. Some extreme weather phenomena, like tornadoes are much less common. But they do occur occasionally in most places, even in Europe – and in some places they are an everyday reality.

Although a tornado is undoubtedly awesome in its power and unpredictability, and it isn't something most people would like to encounter too closely, it still has a visual majesty. There is a reason why people risk their lives to chase these storms – they have a fascination that few other aspects of weather can produce.

Tornado

Rainbow

Dramatic weather can be devastating and dangerous – but it can also be peaceful and beautiful. The rainbow is perhaps the ultimate symbol of the friendly face of the weather. Elusive and impossible to touch, the rainbow brings together the two key elements of weather in rain and sunlight – both of which are essential for our survival, and both of which are key requirements for growing crops or maintaining a garden.

Despite a rainbow being little more than a mirage, a visual trick of the light, it is still something that excites us and brings us together.

Whenever we see a rainbow we feel the desire to point it out to everyone and marvel at the remarkable colours.

The weather is more than a mechanical system, the distribution of air about the planet disrupted and nudged by the energy of the incoming sunlight. It is more than water droplets and photons of light. It is our planet's outer coat, the face it presents to the universe. Seen from space, the characteristic that gives the Earth a uniquely varying appearance is its weather. Weather will always fascinate and frustrate us. Weather phenomena are big and powerful enough to wreck lives and property – but without the weather, life would not be possible.

When you next get a chance, take a look at the red sky that accompanies a setting Sun, the most visible example of the weather's power source interacting with our atmosphere. Without that glorious sight, our lives would be just a little less rich.

Picture credits

Photograph Georg Zumstroll/CC-BY-SA, **p 18**; Courtesy of *Ground Hog Day*, **p 23**; Courtesy of Avogadro's Lab Supply, **p 26b**; Britishbattles.com, **p 32**; Courtesy of NASA/SDO/AIA, **p 66**; Photograph courtesy www.rickety.us/ Creative Commons, **p 88**; © 2004 Twentieth Century Fox Film Corporation, all rights reserved, **p 124**; Courtesy Earth Observatory/NASA, **p 127**; © nico99/ Shutterstock, **p 136**; Courtesy of The Dock Museum/Barrow Borough Council, **p 141**; Courtesy of NASA/JAXA, **p 152**; Courtesy of ASPERA/Novapix/L, **p 161**; Courtesy GISS/NASA, **p 167**.

Illustrations: Jerry Fowler, **pp 10, 28, 40, 69, 70, 74, 76, 80, 81, 94, 104, 123, 133**; Jerry Fowler based on geography.hunter.cuny.edu, **p 30**; Jerry Fowler based on Doofi/Wikimedia Commons, **p 47**; Jerry Fowler based on ellerbruch.nmu. edu, **p 54**; Jerry Fowler based on EPA, **p 67**; Jerry Fowler based on kingfish. coastal.edu/ biology/sgilman/ice, **p 89**; Jerry Fowler based on Ukichiro Nakaya, **p 90**; Jerry Fowler based on NOAA data, **pp 98, 170**; Jerry Fowler based on Leighton Steward, Plants Need CO$_2$, **p 157**.

All Science Photo Library: Jeffrey Greenberg, **frontispiece**; Adrian Bicker, **p 6**; NASA, **pp 9, 12, 39, 103, 105, 156**; Jerry Lodriguss, **p 14**; Mike Boyatt/ AGStockUSA, **p 17**; Tony Craddock, **p 19**; Pekka Parviainen, **pp 21, 58b, 63**; Cape Grim B.A.P.S./Simon Fraser, **p 24**; Library of Congress, **pp 25, 34**; British Crown Copyright, The Met Office, **pp 26, 35**; Dr. John Brackenbury, **pp 27, 76**; Sam Ogden, **p 29**; David R. Frazier Photolibrary, Inc, **p 36**; NASA/Science Source, **p 37**; Michael Donne, **p 41**; Jim Reed, **p 43**; Scott Camazine, **p 45**; John Shaw, **p 48**; Simon Fraser, **pp 51, 112, 174, 183**; Patrick Landmann, **p 52**; Vaughan Fleming, **p 55**; Adam Jones, **p 56**; Joyce Photographics, **p 57**; Pascal Goetgheluck, **p 58t**; Photo Researchers Inc, **p 60**; Ria Novosti, **pp 61, 126**; Dr. Richard Roscoe/Visuals Unlimited, Inc, **pp 62, 125**; Mike Holllingshead, **p 64**; Richard Weymouth Brooks, **p 72**; Kent Wood, **p 75**; Paolo Koch, **p 78**; Cordelia Molloy, **p 79**; Dr. Keith Wheeler, **p 82**; Dr. Rob Stepney, **p 83**; Roger Hill, **p 84**; Ashley Cooper, Visuals Unlimited, **pp 86t, 92**; Alan L. Detrick, **p 86b**; James Steinberg, **p 87**; Kenneth Libbrecht, **p 89**; Tony Craddock, **p 91**; Jim Reed, **p 93**; University Corporation for Atmospheric Research, **p 95**; Jim Edds, **p 97**; Science VU/NASA/GSFC/ Visuals Unlimited, Inc, **p 102**; NOAA, **pp 100, 106, 107, 119, 120**; Chris Butler, **p 108**; Maurice Nimmo, **p 110**; Mark Newman, **p 114**; George Holton, **p 116**; Michael Boyatt/AGSTOCKUSA, **p 117**; Wayne Lawler, **p 118**; George Steinmetz, **p 121**; Kent Wood, **pp 128, 138**; Jim Reed Photography, **pp 130, 147**; Eric Nguyen, **pp 132, 182**; Mike Theiss, **p 134**; Fred

K. Smith, **p 135**; Keith Kent, **p 140**; Jean-Loup Charmet, **p 142**; Sheila Terry, **p 143**; GIPHOTOSTOCK, **p 144**; Andrew Lambert Photography, **p 145**; Peter Menzel, **p 146**; Olivier Vandeginste, **p 148**; Mark Garlick, **p 150**; Equinox Graphics, **p 154**; Chris Madeley, **p 155**; Powell, Fowler & Perkins, **p 159**; Scott Bauer/US Department of Agriculture, **p 161**; Georgette Douwma, **p 162**; Walter Myers, **p 165**; British Antarctic Survey, **p 169**; Thomas Nilsen, **p 171**; Bernard Edmaier, **p 172**; George Steinmetz, **p 173**; Thomas Wiewandt/Visuals Unlimited, Inc, **p 176**; Stephen Harley-Sloman, **p 178**; Mike Hollingshead, **p 180**; Kent Wood, **p 181**; Larry Landolfi, **p 184**.

ACKNOWLEDGEMENTS

Many thanks to Lee Ripley at Vivays Publishing for giving me the opportunity to write this book. I would also like to thank the many staff at the UK Met Office who provided me with large quantities of information when I worked with them a few years ago.

Index

absolute zero 25
Africa 121–2, 124
Agincourt, France 33–4
air circulation 110–11
aircraft 36–7
altocumulus 59
altostratus 59
America *see* South America; US
anemometers 25–6
Antarctica 77, 125, 173
anticyclones 31
Arctic 171
Aristotle 16–17
atmosphere 8, 10–11
    air circulation 110–11
    greenhouse gases 68, 167, 170
    and Sun 67–8
    see also pressure
aurorae 154–5, 158
Australia 118, 120, 121
averages 169

ball lightning 149
balloons 36
Bangladesh 105
barographs 29
barometers 18, 28
Beaufort Scale 111, 113
Bentley, Wilson 88–9
blue skies 20
bombs 110
Brocken spectres 83
butterfly effect, myth of 44

Campbell-Stokes sunshine recorder 27
carbon dioxide 161, 170
    see also greenhouse gases
Celsius scale 25
chaos theory 44–5, 46
Chile 123–4

cirrocumulus 59
cirrostratus 59
cirrus 54, 59
climate 7, 11, 13, 163
modelling 41, 42, 168
climate change 13, 163–73
    causes 167
    debate about 168
    global temperature anomalies
        167–8
    greenhouse effect 161, 165–6, 169
    ice ages 164
    perception of 168–9
    sea level rises 170–1, 173
clouds 49–63
    folk forecasting 20
    impact on climate 161, 168
    seeding 47
    types 53–9
    water droplets 49–52
    wonder of 179
cold fronts 40–1
colour
    clouds 50–3
    rainbows 80–3, 183
    sky 20, 185
communications 157–9
computers 35, 41–2
conduction 66
convection 66
convective rain 77
Coriolis effect 30, 31, 69, 102, 133
coronal mass ejections 153, 156
cosmic rays 159–61
Cowling, George 35
crepuscular rays 53
cumulonimbus 56
cumulus 53, 55–6
cyclones *see* low pressures
cyclonic rain 78

Danakil Depression, Africa 124
deserts 118
dew 85
drizzle 78
droplets 49–52, 74
drought 115–29
    cities 125–9
    impact of 116–19
    predictions 170
    pressure distribution changes
        119–24
dust storms 118–19

El Niño 46, 119–20
energy 65–7
England 7
ensemble forecasts 42–3
Eritrea 124
Ethiopia 124
Europe 122, 126
European Centre for Medium-Range
    Weather Forecasting 42
evaporation 71, 74, 96–7
exosphere 11

Fahrenheit, Daniel 24
Fahrenheit scale 24–5
Faraday cages 146
Ferrel cells 111
fires (wildfires) 117–18, 120
fog 55, 59–61
folk weather forecasting 19–21
forecasting
    computers 35
    history of 15–23, 33–8
    instruments 23–9
    long-range 45–6
    physics of 43–4
France 33–4, 126
Franklin, Benjamin 143–4, 145
frontal rain 77–8
fronts 39–41, 77–8
frost 85–7
frostbite 98

Galton, Francis 35
gases, science of 18
geomagnetic storms 153
glaciers 93, 171
global temperature anomalies 167–8
global thermohaline circulation 122–3
global warming 163, 164, 167
    see also climate change
glories 82
gods 139
gravity 11
greenhouse effect 68, 161, 165–6, 169
greenhouse gases 68, 167, 169
    carbon dioxide 161, 170
Greenland 173
Gulf Stream 122

Hadley cells 111
hail 94–6
Halley's Comet 15
heat waves 126–9, 170
Heisenberg's uncertainty principle 44
high pressures 20, 29–30, 31, 85, 119
highest pressure recorded 29
highest temperatures 124–5
hill fog 60–1
Himalayas 80
history of forecasting 15–23, 33–8
hoar frost 86
Hooke, Robert 29
Howard, Luke 53
human action, and climate change 167
humidity 26–7
hurricanes 101–9
hydrogen bonding 73–4
hygrometers 26–7

ice ages 157, 164
ice cores 169–70
ice crystals 59
ice pellets 94
ice shelves 171, 173
icebergs 93–4
India 80

Indonesia 120, 121
induced charge 144
instruments 23–9
ions 143, 145
Ireland 134

Japan 105
jet streams 68–70
Jupiter 11

Katrina, Hurricane 105
Kelvin scale 25

La Niña 121
leaders (thunderstorms) 145
legends 22–3
Libya 125
light 65–6, 67–8
lightning 139–44, 149
lightning rods 145
'little ice age' 157
long-range forecasting 45–6
Lorenz, Edward 44
low pressures (cyclones)
    bombs 110
    cyclonic rain 78
    hurricanes 104, 105, 107, 109
    Jupiter 11
    nature of 30–1
    winds 113
lowest temperature 125

magnetic field 152–3
Magnus, Olaus 88
manipulating weather intentionally 46–7
Maunder minimum 157
Mayan civilization 115
measurements 23–9
mesosphere 10
Met Office (UK) 33, 35, 36
meteorology 17
mist 55
modelling climate 41, 42, 168
monsoons 78, 80

nature, folk forecasting 20–1
nimbostratus 59
Niña, La 121
Niño, El 46, 119–20
nitrogen 8
noctilucent clouds 59
North America see US
North Atlantic Oscillation 122

occluded fronts 41
oceans 71, 113, 120, 122–3, 170–1, 173
orographic clouds 50
orographic rain 78
oxygen 8
ozone 8, 10

Pacific 120
physics 43–4
Pliocene-Quaternary 164
pluviographs 27
polar cells 110
pressure 27–31
    distribution 77, 119–24
    high 20, 29–30, 31, 85, 119
    low see low pressures
    winds 68
pressure see-saws 119
priests 16

radar 38
radiation 65–6, 67–8
radiation fog 60
radio forecasts 35
rain 73–83
    encouraging 46–7
    fronts 40
    measuring 27
    radar 38
    rainbows 80–3, 183
    raindrops 51–2, 75–6
    types 77–8
    water, nature of 73–4
rainbows 80–3, 183

raindrops 51–2, 75–6
red clouds 52–3
red skies 20, 185
Richardson, Lewis Fry 41
rime frost 86–7

satellites 37–8, 158–9
sea flows 122–3
sea fog 60
sea level rises 170–1, 173
sea spouts 137
seasons 70–1
sky, colour of 20
sleet 94
snow 85, 90–2, 177, 179
snowflakes 87–90
solar storms 153, 158
solar wind 151, 153, 154, 157, 159
South America 121, 123–4
Spanish Armada 34
Stevenson, Thomas 23
Stevenson Screens 23
storm surges 105–7
stratocumulus 56
stratopause 10
stratosphere 8, 10
stratus 54, 55
stratus fractus 55
Sullivan, Roy 141
Sun 65–71
    appearance of 20
    atmosphere of 151
    coronal mass ejections 153,
        156
sunshine 27
sunspots 156–7
supercells 147

telegraph, electric 34–5, 158
television forecasts 35
temperature 23–5, 124–5, 167–8
thermals 50, 56, 131, 133
thermohaline circulation 122–3
thermometers 18, 24

thermosphere 11
thunder 146
thunderheads 56
thunderstones 140–1
thunderstorms 139–49
    cities 129
    lightning 139–44, 149
    risk reduction 145–6
    thunderheads 56
    volcanic storms 147, 149
    wonder of 179–81
tornadoes 131–7, 182
Tower of the Winds 18
trade winds 77, 120
tropopause 8
troposphere 8
tsunamis 107–8
twisters 131
typhoons 104

UK 7, 137
units, measurements 24
urban heat islands 125–9
US 121, 127–8, 134, 137

Venus 11, 166
volcanic storms 147, 149
volcanoes 61–2
von Neumann, John 41

warm fronts 39–40
Wasaburo Ooishi 69
water 16, 49–52, 73–4
    see also clouds; oceans; rain
water vapour 74
waves, ocean 113
weather
definition 7–8
wonder of 177–85
weather charts 35
weather stations 23–9, 36
wind chill 96, 98–9
wind speed 25–6
wind vanes 18

winds 68–70
    Beaufort Scale 111, 113
    monsoons 78, 80
    trade winds 77, 120
    wind chill 96, 98–9
    wind speed 25–6
    wind vanes 18
witches 16